D1234644

the Friends of the
Public Library
of SAINT PAUL,
Minnesota, inc.
GIFT

JOHN F. and MYRTLE V.

BRIGGS

CHARITABLE TRUST

BREVET'S

NEBRASKA

HISTORICAL

MARKERS

and

SITES

F
667
B73

C56943

ST. PAUL PUBLIC LIBRARY

Published By Brevet Press

Copyright © 1974 by BREVET PRESS,
a division of BREVET INTERNATIONAL, INC.
410 Northwestern Bank Building, Sioux Falls,
South Dakota 57102

Library of Congress Catalog Card Number: 74-79979

Hard Cover Edition
ISBN: 0-88498-020-0

Soft Cover Edition
ISBN: 0-88498-021-9

All rights reserved.
No part of this work nor its format covered by the
copyright hereon may be reproduced or used in any
form or by any means - graphic, electronic or
mechanical, including photocopying, recording,
taping or information storage retrieval systems -
without written permission of the publisher.

First Printing 1974
Manufactured in the United States of America

ST. PAUL PUBLIC LIBRARY

Editor

N. Jane Hunt

Publisher: Donald P. Mackintosh
Managing Editor: Blake R. Kellogg
Consulting Editor: Tom Kakonis
Cover Art: Don Steinbeck
Page Art, Maps and Marker Design: Gail J. Smith and John Caverly
Printing: Sanders Printing Company, Garretson, South Dakota

NEBRASKA HISTORIC MARKERS

The marking of significant historic sites and events has been a program of the Nebraska State Historical Society since 1909 when Robert Harvey surveyed the Oregon Trail through Nebraska. With the assistance of a state appropriation and private funds, particularly from the Daughters of the American Revolution, the Society erected a series of granite markers along this important migration route.

Marker efforts were largely uncoordinated until 1957 when the Nebraska Legislature formed the Historic Land Mark Committee. The Historic Land Mark Commission was formed in 1959, and in 1969 the Nebraska State Historical Society was assigned the responsibility for erecting uniform historical markers along Nebraska's highways and at important sites. The Society is also responsible for approving the content of historical markers erected by private groups or individuals.

Since 1963 over 160 markers have been erected throughout the state. Most are five-by-six foot cast aluminum markers containing about 180 words. Markers are usually erected on a matching fund basis, with local organizations assuming 50 percent of purchase costs. In many rest areas along the Interstate Highway system, built-in markers serve to educate travelers on the history of our state. The State Department of Roads has been instrumental in the success of this program, assuming costs of erection for markers located in turnouts or wayside areas along our state highway system. In the near future, the Nebraska State Historical Society will offer a smaller marker to be placed at the sites of important buildings and structures.

Marvin F. Kivett
Director, Nebraska State Historical Society

ACKNOWLEDGMENTS

The editors wish to acknowledge each of several persons who gave generously of their time and talents. Their untiring efforts facilitated the creation of this book.

First acknowledgment must go to Marvin F. Kivett, director of the Nebraska State Historical Society. His talent, knowledge and quiet leadership account heavily for the success of the Society in preserving Nebraska history. His knowledge of Nebraska's past is substantial and he always produced the correct answers to our many questions.

The Nebraska State Historical Society is staffed with experts who master the separate disciplines. One of these is Opal Jacobsen, Photographic Librarian. She and her assistant, Kathy Kennedy, helped locate the right illustrations, often with a serving of gentle humor.

Another, Wendell Frantz, the Nebraska State Historical Museum Curator, also generously supplied photographs about the museum and its displays.

The Department of Economic Development has a very able Facilities Development Director, Gary Toebben, who more than once located needed information and photographs.

Foremost among those who lent their services towards the book from the Nebraska Game and Parks Commission is Ted Stutheit, the chief of the State Parks Division. He found not only photographs, but also names and locations for more illustrations and data once his resources were spent.

One of the last persons to open her files of illustrations and historical data, but certainly not the least, is Betty M. White, Public Information Specialist of the National Park Service. She knows Nebraska's national monuments and their visitors well.

To all these persons, a final tribute must be paid to Nebraska's proud history told by her historical highway markers, historical parks, museums, monuments and, finally, by her people.

The Editors

Contents

Eastern Nebraska

Contents

The Sandhills and Central Nebraska

Nebraska's Panhandle

Map Key

To assist the reader, the state of Nebraska has been divided into three geographic parts. This book follows the geographical divisions - each with its own color key. The color keyed maps indicate the position of the marker or historical site in the state.

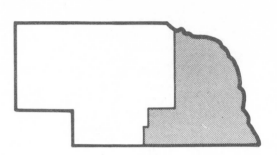

BLUE
Eastern Nebraska

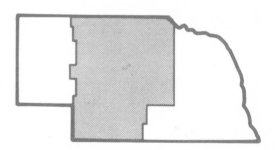

GREEN
The Sandhills and Central Nebraska

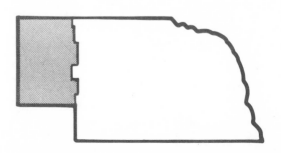

BROWN
Nebraska's Panhandle

NEBRASKA
HISTORICAL MARKER

EASTERN

NEBRASKA

NEBRASKA
HISTORICAL MARKER

THE OREGON TRAIL

The most traveled of the overland routes passed this point on its way to the great Platte valley, highway to the west. The Oregon Trail started from Independence, followed the Kansas River west, and then the Little Blue north into Nebraska. It crossed this divide to reach the Platte near Fort Kearny.

In the 1830's trappers and missionaries recognized the Platte valley as a natural roadway. The first wagon train followed the 2,000-mile trail to Oregon in 1841.

An estimated quarter of a million travelers used this route in the twenty-five years after those first wagons. Moving slowly, only 10 to 20 miles a day on the three-month trip, thousands of hooves, shoes, and wheels pounded a wide trail into the prairie sod.

Oregon was an early goal. The '49'ers went this way to California. Settlers, stage coaches, freighting wagons, Pony Express riders, and military expeditions all used this prairie highway.

With completion of the Union Pacific Railroad in 1869, this route fell into disuse, but the Oregon Trail had earned a permanent place in our history.

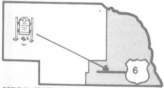

OFFICIAL STATE MAP: L-21
ADAMS COUNTY

Located: US 6 - 6 miles west of Hastings.

With Chimney Rock in the distance, this W.H. Jackson painting depicts the hey-day of the Oregon Trail.

Nebraska State Historical Society

Nebraska State Historical Society
Joseph William Spirk

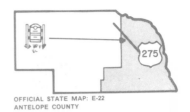

OFFICIAL STATE MAP: E-22
ANTELOPE COUNTY

Located: US 275 at Neligh, north of old mill.

NEBRASKA
HISTORICAL MARKER

THE NELIGH MILLS

The Neligh Mills, built from locally fired brick in 1873 by John D. Neligh, was the first business and industry in the then newly platted town. Later owners and operators of the mill included William C. Galloway, Stephen F. Gilman and J. W. Spirk. Milling operations began in 1874 with two runs of stone. Roller mills were added in 1878, and all new roller mills were installed in 1898. Flour from the Neligh Mills was widely sold throughout the Middle West. Better known brands produced here include Neligh Patent Flour, So-Lite Flour and Crescent brand feeds.

A good mill was a major factor in the growth of Nebraska communities during the 1870's and 1880's. Mills turned locally grown grain into flour, cutting down on expensive long distance shipping. Mills with an ample water supply and situated on main rail lines were able to produce quantities in excess of local needs, and sometimes received lucrative government contracts with the Army and Indian Bureau or for overseas export.

In 1969 the Legislature authorized the Nebraska State Historical Society to acquire and preserve this mill as a symbol of our agricultural history. Its importance was also recognized in 1969 by entry on the National Register of Historic Places.

The Neligh Mills as they are today
Nebraska State Historical Society

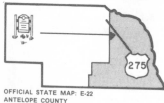

OFFICIAL STATE MAP: E-22
ANTELOPE COUNTY

Located: US 275 - ½ mile north and 2 blocks east at Neligh Cemetery.

NEBRASKA
HISTORICAL MARKER

PONCA TRAIL OF TEARS
WHITE BUFFALO GIRL

A marker, 200 feet to the south, recalls the death of White Buffalo Girl of the Ponca tribe. The death of this child, daughter of Black Elk and Moon Hawk, symbolizes the tragic 1877 removal of the Ponca from their homeland on the Niobrara River to Indian Territory in present Oklahoma.

Treaties in 1858 and 1865 greatly reduced the size of the original Ponca Reservation, yet the tribe remained peaceful. An 1868 error in the Treaty of Fort Laramie ceded Ponca lands to their enemy the Dakota Sioux, resulting in eight years of repeated raids against the Ponca and ending with the forced removal of the tribe to the new reservation.

The journey to Indian Territory was plagued by muddy roads and floods caused by heavy spring rains. Most of the tribe suffered from disease and hardship. Several children like White Buffalo Girl perished and were buried along this route that became known as the Ponca "Trail of Tears." The people of Neligh provided a Christian funeral for the child and an oak cross was erected at the gravesite. Black Elk's last request was that the grave of his daughter would be honored and cared for by the people of the town. In 1913 a marble monument was erected and the grave has been maintained and decorated in memory of White Buffalo Girl and the Ponca.

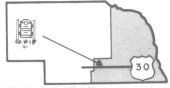

OFFICIAL STATE MAP: L-20
BUFFALO COUNTY

Located: US 30 - 3½ miles south of Gibbon on Windmill Wayside Park 10c link of I-80.

Nebraska State Historical Society
Brevet Major General John Gibbon

NEBRASKA
HISTORICAL MARKER

1871 GIBBON 1971

Gibbon, on the old Mormon Trail, was the site of a unique experiment in homestead colonization. Originally conceived as a financial venture by Colonel John Thorp of Ohio, the Soldier's Free Homestead Colony was responsible for bringing the first homesteaders to the region. Traveling by Union Pacific, which had reached this point in July 1866, the first group of colonists, representing 80 families, arrived in Gibbon on April 7, 1871.

Thorp had advertised for colonists, charging a membership fee of $2.00, with which they received reduced railroad rates to Gibbon, where it was expected that the Civil War Veterans would purchase railroad land and take homesteads, thus increasing the value of other nearby railroad lands.

When the first colonists arrived at Gibbon siding, named for Civil War General John Gibbon, the only building was a small section house, and, until sod or frame homes could be built, they lived in railroad box cars. Later arrivals increased the original colonists to 129 families from 15 states, all but a few being Union veterans.

The settlers' first view of the area was not encouraging as a prairie fire had recently swept over the region, leaving charred desolation in its wake. Two days after their arrival, a two-day blizzard struck the area. It is a tribute to the perseverance of these hardy pioneers that only one colonist failed to file a homestead claim.

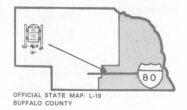

OFFICIAL STATE MAP: L-19
BUFFALO COUNTY

Located: 11th Street in Kearney Centenniel Park.

Nebraska State Historical Society

Brigham Young appeared in this 1855 daguerreotype.

NEBRASKA
HISTORICAL MARKER

HISTORIC KEARNEY

In 1847 Brigham Young led the first migration over the Morman Trail along the north bank of the Platte River, and in 1866 the Union Pacific Railroad pushed its main line westward to this valley, bringing pioneer settlers. However, it was not until 1871 when the Burlington & Missouri River Railroad fixed the junction point of its line with the Union Pacific that a townsite was established here.

The village of Kearney Junction was platted in the summer of 1871 and the junction of the two railroads was completed on September 18, 1872. In the fall of 1873, a bridge was completed across the Platte, connecting Kearney with the rapidly developing areas to the south. The City of Kearney was incorporated on December 3, 1873, and became the county seat of Buffalo County in 1874.

Kearney developed rapidly as an industrial, agricultural, and cultural center. The railroads and the promise of industry offered by the new Kearney Canal, which was completed in 1886, brought many investors from the East, and by 1892 the population reached the 10,000 mark. This golden era launched the Kearney Cotton Mill, the famed 1733 Ranch, a splendid five-story opera house, and one of the state's first electric street railways.

Located: Highway 30, west of Kearney.

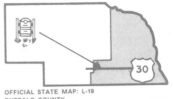

OFFICIAL STATE MAP: L-19
BUFFALO COUNTY

NEBRASKA
HISTORICAL MARKER

KEARNEY COTTON MILL

In the late 1880's, Kearney business leaders envisioned the city as a major manufacturing center. The Kearney Cotton Mill was among the many enterprises launched as part of this venture, which included paper, woolen, and oatmeal mills; plow and canning factories; brick works and machine shops. The economic depression of the early 1890's, however, ended most of these businesses.

The Kearney Cotton Mill was financed in part by a Massachusetts firm. Upon its completion in 1892 the mill was the largest manufacturing plant in Nebraska. The two-story brick structure cost over $400,000 to construct. Raw cotton was shipped from the South by barge and railroad. At peak efficiency the mill employed about 450 workers and produced 26,000 yards of unbleached muslin daily, some of which was shipped to such faraway places as the Orient.

In 1901 the plant was closed due to economic pressures, including high freight rates and labor costs. During its existence the mill never operated at a profit. The building stood vacant until the Midway Amusement Park was established in the spring of 1920. A swimming pool was constructed in the basement of the plant and the main building was used as a dance pavilion. On March 18, 1922, the mill and park facilities were destroyed by fire.

The Kearney Cotton Mills' Interior

Nebraska State Historical Society

Nebraska State Historical Society

This historic drawing of the State Normal School at Kearney showed the proposed wings of the building.

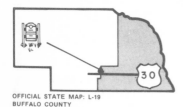

OFFICIAL STATE MAP: L-19
BUFFALO COUNTY

Located: US 30 - on Kearney State College campus.

NEBRASKA
HISTORICAL MARKER

KEARNEY STATE COLLEGE

In January, 1903, the Legislature of the State of Nebraska appropriated $50,000 for the establishment of a State Normal School to be located in central or western Nebraska. On the 111th ballot, the Nebraska State Board of Education selected Kearney as the site and construction of the Administration Building started in 1904.

The new institution was located on a site of some 20 acres on the west edge of Kearney. The location included one building, Green Terrace Hall, which was used mainly as a dormitory until razed in 1960.

The first classes of Kearney State Normal School were held in the summer of 1905 with 96 students enrolled. The name of the school was changed in 1921 to Nebraska State Teachers College at Kearney and the program was expanded from two to four years. In 1949, the College was authorized to grant Liberal Arts degrees and in 1956 to establish a graduate program. The official name of the institution was changed to Kearney State College in 1963. As an institution of higher education the College performed an important role in the development of the State and continues to meet the educational, research, and service needs of the State of Nebraska.

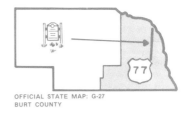

OFFICIAL STATE MAP: G-27
BURT COUNTY

Located: US 77 between Oakland and Vehling.

Nebraska State Historical Society

Logan Fontenelle, Chief of the Omaha

NEBRASKA
HISTORICAL MARKER

THE LOGAN CREEK SITE

Logan Creek was named for Logan Fontenelle, a chief of the Omaha tribe killed by Oglala Sioux in 1855. The first recorded settlers in this area were the Aaron Arlington family, 1857, who settled at the site of present Oakland, and John Oak, 1862, for whom the town was named. The Logan Creek archeological site, located on a nearby stream terrace, was investigated by the Nebraska State Historical Society, 1957-1963 with the aid of a National Science Foundation grant.

Nine stratified cultural zones, extending a depth of nearly 12 feet, have been defined. The uppermost zone is attributed to a Plains Woodland people--the first pottery makers in Nebraska, believed to have migrated from Eastern Woodlands. At least five of the lower zones may represent a distinct culture, known as the Logan Creek Complex. Carbon 14 dates indicate these closely related groups periodically camped here between 6000 and 8000 years ago. The water, good hunting and fresh water shell fish may have been some of the reasons for the long inhabitation by these hunting, fishing and gathering people.

Artifacts from this site show close cultural ties with contemporary Archaic cultures in eastern and northeast America. The findings here are the earliest excavated human materials yet discovered in eastern Nebraska. In 1970 the Logan Creek Site was entered on the National Register of Historic Places.

LYONS

The first settlers of Lyons came in the summer of 1866. The fertile soil of the Logan Valley, combined with the commercial promise provided by access to the railroad after 1881, assured the life of the town. Incorporated in 1884, the village was named for Waldo Lyon, a prominent citizen upon whose land the plots were laid out. Residents have continued to abide by a provision in Lyon's deed, stipulating that liquor not be sold within the town at risk of forfeit of the property.

The Lyons Roller Mill was erected in 1869. The three-story structure was powered by water from a dam built across Logan Creek just west of the town, and was in operation until 1931.

Many of the buildings of the town are constructed of brick manufactured in a brick yard which began operation in 1878. The swimming pool sits in the depression from which the clay was taken.

One of the finest trotting tracks in the country opened in 1891, just one-fourth mile west of Lyons, named The Kite Track. Famous horses broke world records and won large purses on this kite-shaped race track before hard times ended racing after 1893.

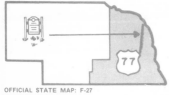

OFFICIAL STATE MAP: F-27
BURT COUNTY

Located: US 77 - southern edge of Lyons, west side of highway.

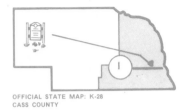

OFFICIAL STATE MAP: K-28
CASS COUNTY

Located: Nebraska 1 - Elmwood Park in Elmwood.

Nebraska State Historical Society Bess Streeter Aldrich

NEBRASKA
HISTORICAL MARKER

BESS STREETER ALDRICH
1881-1954

"Love is more like a light that you carry .... that is what love is to a woman - a lantern in her hand," says Abbie Deal the courageous heroine in Bess Streeter Aldrich's novel about the pioneers who with dreams and hard work forged this great State of Nebraska. This memorable work became a veritable text-book of life on the prairie, the development of Nebraska; it was translated into many foreign languages.

THE RIM OF THE PRAIRIE, A LANTERN IN HER HAND, A WHITE BIRD FLYING, MISS BISHOP, SPRING CAME ON FOREVER and **SONG OF YEARS** are remembered among her many stories of family life.

Bess Streeter Aldrich was born in Cedar Falls, Iowa, was educated at Iowa State Teachers College, taught school in Iowa and Utah, married Captain Charles S. Aldrich, settled in Elmwood and raised their four children.

Mrs. Aldrich portrayed life with a cheerful realism which set her apart from most other writers of the time. Her immense popularity as an author was due not only to her ability to convey life on the prairie most vividly but also to the delicate touch by which she portrayed the warmth, feelings, and personality of her characters.

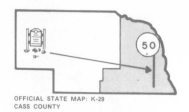

OFFICIAL STATE MAP: K-29
CASS COUNTY

Located: Nebraska 50 - east into Weeping Water, 2 blocks east of post office at Weeping Water Public Library.

Nebraska State Historical Society
Mr. and Mrs. George Hindley

NEBRASKA
HISTORICAL MARKER

WEEPING WATER ACADEMY

This building was constructed by community effort in 1871 of native limestone as the Congregational Church and served in that capacity until a new brick church was constructed 1887-1890. The nearby stone parsonage, first occupied in 1867, was sold in 1870 to provide funds for the 1871 church.

The old church provided space for the chapel, classrooms, and library for the Weeping Water Academy which was established in 1885, as its founders felt their children could not receive adequate training in the local public schools of the day. An active promoter of the school was the Rev. George Hindley. Due to his efforts, the school became and remained identified with the Congregationalists, although the work was largely nondenominational. Three formal courses of study were offered including classical, scientific and English Normal.

As enrollment increased, other buildings were utilized or constructed with the largest being Hindley Cottage. The school closed in June, 1914, due to decreased enrollment as public schools improved. During its 29 years of existence, the academy had some 220 graduates. In 1917 this building became the "Weeping Water Academy Library" and continues to serve as the public library today.

Hindley Cottage, Weeping Water Academy
Nebraska State Historical Society

Nebraska State Historical Society

Main Street of Early Edgar

Located: Nebraska 14 - north
side of 5th Street between F
and G Avenues in Edgar.

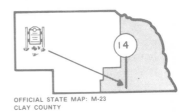

OFFICIAL STATE MAP: M-23
CLAY COUNTY

NEBRASKA
HISTORICAL MARKER

1872 EDGAR 1972

Edgar lies in the Little Blue River Valley just north of the old Oregon and California trails. The townsite was pre-empted in March 1872 by Henry Gipe with funds provided by the Nebraska Land and Townsite Company. The first post office was established in June of that year in a log cabin on the A. J. Ritterbush farm. One month later the St. Joseph and Denver City Railroad completed tracks into the area and laid out the town of Eden, which later became Edgar. The town was surveyed in May 1873.

Edgar was incorporated on March 15, 1875. The droughts and grasshopper plagues of the middle 1870's slowed the development of the community temporarily, but by 1880 the population had grown to nearly 600. The 1886 coming of the Nebraska and Colorado Railroad, part of the Burlington system, assisted the community's rise as a manufacturing center. At its height Edgar had a creamery, a brick and tile company, a cannery, and several mills. The farm depression of the 1890's, however, signaled an end of growth for the town.

Edgar today is a quiet community and remains a part of the great American agricultural heartland. Although its role as a service center for the area has declined, the people of Edgar carry the proud traditions and the rugged spirit of their pioneer ancestors.

Nebraska State Historical Society

Luther French, founder of Sutton, settled on his Nebraska homestead March 14, 1870.

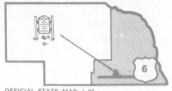

OFFICIAL STATE MAP: L-23
CLAY COUNTY

Located: US 6 - Sutton near pavilion at Sutton City Park.

NEBRASKA
HISTORICAL MARKER

SUTTON

The first permanent settler in the town of Sutton was Luther French, who arrived in 1870. He and his seven children lived near here in a dugout on the bank of School Creek. This dugout had a tunnel to the creek bank; the inside entrance could be concealed by a crude cupboard. In the event of an Indian attack, the children were instructed to take cover in the tunnel. Apparently, Indians never bothered the family.

In 1871 the French homestead was laid out as a townsite and named for Sutton, Massachusetts. Soon after its founding, the town found itself engaged in conflict with the Burlington and Missouri Railroad. Sutton wished to have a depot and offered land for the construction of facilities. Because the title to the Sutton land was not clear, the railroad located its depot 4½ miles from Sutton and laid out a townsite there. By 1873, the railroad had decided to relocate the depot in Sutton.

This area was hard hit by the grasshopper plague of 1874. Sutton became a distribution center for federal, state and private aid. Without this aid, many settlers might not have survived the following winter.

Sutton Street, Sutton, as viewed from railroad tracks looking south

Nebraska State Historical Society

Nebraska State Historical Society

John G. Neihardt, Author, Editor and Poet

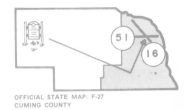

OFFICIAL STATE MAP: F-27
CUMING COUNTY

Located: ½ mile west of intersection of Nebraska 51 and 16, eastern side of Bancroft.

NEBRASKA HISTORICAL MARKER

BANCROFT

Bancroft was the home of John G. Neihardt between 1900 and 1920. Here he wrote all of his short stories and lyric poetry including **A Bundle of Myrrh. The Splendid Wayfaring**, and the **Guest** and began his epic poem **A Cycle of the West** which brought him high critical acclaim.

Born in Illinois January 3, 1881, Neihardt lived in Kansas and Missouri before settling in Wayne, Nebraska in 1892. He began writing poetry at the age of twelve, worked his way through Nebraska Normal College at Wayne and taught school. In Bancroft he worked for an Indian trader and edited the **Bancroft Blade**. In 1921 he was appointed Poet Laureate of Nebraska by Legislative Act.

Many Omaha Indians in the Bancroft vicinity helped the poet gain his profound understanding and compassion for their race. Among them were Dr. Susan La Flesche Picotte and her sister Susette (Bright Eyes), daughter of Joseph La Flesche (Iron Eyes) last recognized chief of the Omaha. Susette, an eloquent and attractive speaker, was famous for her tireless and effective work in behalf of her people. She is buried beside her father and mother in the Bancroft cemetery.

COMBS SCHOOL
Built 1857 - Closed 1964

The frame schoolhouse in the background is part of Nebraska's pioneer heritage - the oldest school building in Dakota County and one of the oldest in Nebraska.

Originally erected in the spring of 1857 at Omadi, four miles south of Dakota City, the school shared the townsite's peril when the Missouri River began to undermine the area. Since the school faced destruction it was moved to Thomas Smith's claim, about two miles south of Homer. Here a new school district was organized.

When construction on the Burlington railroad from Sioux City to Lincoln began, the school was found to be on railroad property. The building was then shifted to its present site near the old Combs mill. School redistricting eliminated need for the old Combs School, and its doors closed for the last time May 22, 1964.

The Board of Education of the newly-formed district donated the building to the Dakota County Historical Society, who has set it aside as a monument to the pioneer fathers' belief that, "MEN ARE ENNOBLED BY UNDERSTANDING."

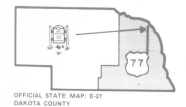

OFFICIAL STATE MAP: E-27
DAKOTA COUNTY

Located: US 77 - 2 miles south of Homer.

The Combs School as it appears in 1974

Brevet Press

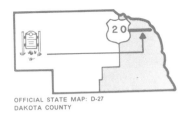

OFFICIAL STATE MAP: D-27
DAKOTA COUNTY

Located: US 20 - in front of St. Patrick's Church in Jackson.

Brevet Press

St. Peter's Catholic Church in Jackson

NEBRASKA
HISTORICAL MARKER

ST. JOHN'S
1856

About 1½ miles north of this spot is the abandoned site of "Old St. John's", one of the first towns established in Dakota County.

The townsite was settled on June 2, 1856, by the Father Trecy Colony--sixty people, with eighteen ox-drawn covered wagons. The site was surveyed and platted June 24, 1856, and the town was named St. John's, in honor of St. John the Baptist.

The Colony was led by Father Jeremiah Trecy, a young Catholic Priest from the Garryowen Parish near Dubuque, Iowa. Consisting mostly of Irish immigrants, it constituted the first Catholic parish in Nebraska. The town of St. John's grew rapidly and by 1858 it had two hundred inhabitants.

In 1860 Father Trecy went to Washington seeking permission to establish a mission among the Ponca Indians. Meanwhile the Civil War began. Father Trecy became an army chaplain, and never returned to his beloved Colony.

In the early sixties, the Missouri River began to threaten St. John's. The people began moving their buildings to the new town of Jackson. By 1866 all buildings were gone and the townsite was abandoned.

The site of St. John's still exists as a symbol of courage, and hope and of the religious faith of a dedicated people.

Nebraska State Historical Society
Emmanuel Lutheran Church

Nebraska State Historical Society
The Rev. H.W. Kuhns DD

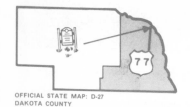

OFFICIAL STATE MAP: D-27
DAKOTA COUNTY

Located: US 73 - 77 - 2 blocks south on 15th Street in Dakota City.

NEBRASKA
HISTORICAL MARKER

TERRITORIAL CHURCH

Near here stands the first Lutheran church building constructed in Nebraska. It has occupied this site since 1860.

The congregation was first served by Reverend Henry W. Kuhns, a missionary sent by the Allegheny Synod to Nebraska Territory. Kuhns preached his first sermon in the front room of the Bates House (hotel) in November 1858 and formally organized the church on July 22, 1859.

The membership immediately made plans for building, but their first effort of moving an abandoned store from the abandoned town of Pacific City was frustrated when the structure was destroyed by a prairie fire while being moved to Dakota City.

This church was designed and built by Augustus T. Haase, a local carpenter and member of the Emmanuel Lutheran congregation, at a cost of $2,000. For several years the building also served periodically as a Territorial courthouse, with religious services being held on Sunday as usual. Samuel Aughey, a leading scientist of the period, was the second pastor to serve the church.

This old church still stands as a monument to the steadfastness of purpose of the early settler and as a symbol of pioneer religious life.

Located: US 77 - 1 mile north of Homer.

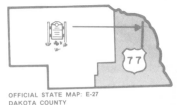

OFFICIAL STATE MAP: E-27
DAKOTA COUNTY

NEBRASKA
HISTORICAL MARKER

TONWANTONGA

An important Omaha Indian village called Tonwantonga (Large Village) by the Omaha stood on Omaha Creek in this area. Ruled by the great chief Blackbird, an estimated 1,100 people lived in this earthlodge town about 1795 and it played an important role in Indian and exploratory history.

Many explorers and fur traders visited this spot before 1800. Near it the Spanish built a fort, armed it with heavy guns, and named it Fort Charles honoring Charles IV.

The Lewis and Clark expedition visited the village August 13, 1804, finding it deserted, as the Omaha were away on an extended buffalo hunt. The explorers stayed near the site for a week and held a conference with three chiefs of the Oto tribe who had come to make peace with the absent Omaha.

In 1800 disaster had struck the village as smallpox killed an estimated 400 including the famous Chief Blackbird. After Blackbird's death the village ceased to play so important a role in the struggle for control of the Missouri Valley and the Plains beyond.

Captains Lewis and Clark held council with Oto chiefs during the Omahas absence.
Nebraska State Historical Society

19

NEBRASKA
HISTORICAL MARKER

THE IONIA "VOLCANO"

On August 24, 1804, the Lewis and Clark Expedition, traveling up the Missouri River, passed a bluff about 180 to 190 feet high. Clark wrote that it appeared to have been on fire and was still very hot. He also detected signs of coal and what looked like cobalt. Later fur traders frequently noticed dense smoke and fire in this region. In 1839, J. N. Nicollet attempted to prove that these phenomena were not of volcanic origin. Nicollet theorized that the decomposition of beds of iron pyrites in contact with water resulted in a heat capable of igniting other combustible materials.

Unaware of this explanation, early settlers continued to fear the "Ionia volcano," which took its name from the once flourishing town of Ionia, located northeast of present-day Newcastle. An earthquake in 1877 aroused new fears of an impending volcanic eruption. In 1878, the Missouri River undermined the bluffs and a large section of the "volcano" fell into the river. The same flood nearly destroyed the town of Ionia. "Volcano" stories died out soon after the Ionia post office was discontinued in 1907.

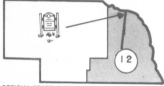

OFFICIAL STATE MAP: C-26
DIXON COUNTY

Located: Nebraska 12 - Pfister Park eastern edge of Newcastle.

Nebraska State Historical Society

Historic newspaper engraving of a delegation of Ponca chiefs

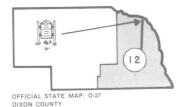

OFFICIAL STATE MAP: D-27
DIXON COUNTY

Located: Main Street of Ponca.

NEBRASKA
HISTORICAL MARKER

PONCA

Ponca, one of northeast Nebraska's earliest communities, was platted in 1856 by Frank West and laid out by Dr. Solomon B. Stough. The town was named for the Ponca Indian tribe that inhabited the area when the first white settlers arrived. The location provided an abundant supply of wood and water.

Originally part of Dakota County, Ponca was named as the seat of government when Dixon County was organized by the Territorial Legislature in 1858. The first county business was conducted in the Frank Ricker and Brothers general store. Water power from the Aowa Creek basin contributed significantly to the early growth of the community, which boasted flour and saw mills by 1861. Development slowed during the Civil War and the grasshopper plagues of the 1870's. The 1876 completion of the Covington, Columbus and Black Hills Railroad, the county's first, marked the beginning of a new era of economic growth. During the 1890's Ponca sported one of the finest one-mile thoroughbred racetracks in the Midwest.

In 1934 the Civilian Conservation Corps began the development of the original 220-acre site of Ponca State Park on the banks of the Missouri River. This park has become one of Nebraska's finest outdoor recreation areas.

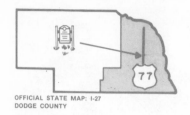

OFFICIAL STATE MAP: I-27
DODGE COUNTY

Located: US 77 - wayside
park south of Platte River.

Nebraska State Historical Society
General John M. Thayer

NEBRASKA
HISTORICAL MARKER

PAWNEE VILLAGES

Before the Pawnee Indians were placed on a reservation, they located their last earth lodge villages on these nearby bluffs. **Pa-huk'** hill, one of the five sacred places of the Pawnee, was also here. The villages were occupied from 1850 to 1859 by the Skidi, Tappage and Grand bands led by head chief Petalesharo. The Republican band lived some distance up stream.

The Pawnee once numbered more than 10,000 people and were recorded in history as early as 1541. Often harassed by the Sioux, they erected sod walls to protect their villages. The Pawnee were friendly toward whites, and some later served as army scouts.

By 1833 the tribe had given up all of its land north of the Platte River. General John M. Thayer and O. D. Richardson, representing Territorial Governor Izard, held a conference with the tribe here in 1855. In 1857 the Indians signed the Treaty of Table Creek, ceding the rest of their land to the whites. In return they received a reservation along the Loup River near present-day Genoa. In 1875 the Pawnee moved south to Indian Territory, ending their settlement in Nebraska.

OFFICIAL STATE MAP: I-29
DOUGLAS COUNTY

Located: US 73 - 8500 block on north 30th Street in Florence, Omaha.

Nebraska State Historical Society **Bank of Florence**

NEBRASKA
HISTORICAL MARKER

THE BANK OF FLORENCE

The Bank of Florence was chartered by the Nebraska Territorial legislature on January 18, 1856. It was located in this substantial building, constructed during the same year. Sheet steel one quarter inch thick, shipped by river steamboat from Pennsylvania steel mills, was used in conjunction with three foot thick masonry to build the vault.

The bank was owned and operated by the respected Iowa financial firm of Cook and Sargent. It played an important role in the aspiration of the town of Florence to become the leading transportation and financial center of Nebraska. Frontier banking practices were lax and along with other banks in Nebraska Territory the Bank of Florence issued quantities of unsecured "wild cat" currency and financed speculation in land. Weakened by the financial panic of 1857 the Bank failed in 1859. Only one bank in Nebraska territory survived the Panic.

The building housed a variety of subsequent business operations including a second Bank of Florence which was chartered in 1904. It is now restored as it appeared in territorial times.

Nebraska State Historical Society **Interior of Bank of Florence**

Nebraska State Historical Society

The Steamer Omaha landed Mormons at Florence in the Spring of 1854

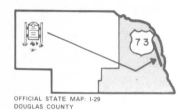

OFFICIAL STATE MAP: I-29
DOUGLAS COUNTY

Located: US 73 - 1 block east
of intersection of 73 and 36,
east of mill.

NEBRASKA
HISTORICAL MARKER

THE FLORENCE MILL

The Florence Mill, one of the earliest in Nebraska, was constructed by the Mormons at Winter Quarters during the winter of 1846-1847. Supplying both flour and lumber, the water-powered mill enabled the Mormons to cope more readily with the adverse conditions encountered during their stay in Nebraska. In 1847-1848 groups of Mormons began to leave this area for the Salt Lake Valley, and as a result, Winter Quarters and the mill were abandoned.

In 1856, Alexander Hunter began to operate the mill. Its products helped fill the demands created by the growing town of Florence, established in 1854 on the old site of Winter Quarters.

By 1870, Jacob Weber had acquired the operation. Flour became its most important product, and by 1880 steam had largely replaced water as the motive force. The mill was further modified in later years to meet changing demands, and it continued to operate under the direction of second and third generation members of the Weber family.

Spanning more than a century, the history of the Florence Mill reflects the important contribution of the milling industry to the development of Nebraska.

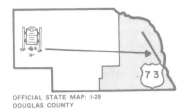

OFFICIAL STATE MAP: I-29
DOUGLAS COUNTY

Located: US 73 - Florence
Park, Omaha.

Nebraska State Historical Society
Winter Quarters Monument

NEBRASKA HISTORICAL MARKER

WINTER QUARTERS

Here in 1846 an oppressed people fleeing from a vengeful mob found a haven in the wilderness. Winter Quarters, established under the direction of the Mormon leader Brigham Young, sheltered more than 3,000 people during the winter of 1846-1847. Housed in log cabins, sod houses and dugouts, they lacked adequate provisions. When spring arrived more than six hundred of the faithful lay buried in the cemetery on the hill. Winter Quarters became the administration center of a great religious movement.

In the spring of 1847 a pioneer band left Winter Quarters to cross the Plains to the Great Salt Lake Valley. Thousands of others followed this trail. In 1855, Young was forced to utilize handcarts for transportation. The first company, comprising about five hundred persons, left here on July 17 and reached the Valley on September 26, 1856.

The town of Florence, established in 1854, was built upon the site of Winter Quarters. James C. Mitchell and Associates of the Florence Land Company established a thriving community. The Bank of Florence, built in 1856, stands today as a symbol of our historical past.

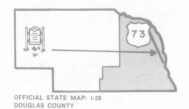

Located: US 73 - 75 - 24th Street southbound at California Street in Omaha.

NEBRASKA
HISTORICAL MARKER

CREIGHTON UNIVERSITY

This University is named for Edward and John A. Creighton -- Ohio farm boys who gained immortality in the West. They helped to link our coasts by telegraph during the Civil War. They pioneered as cattlemen on the Laramie Plains, as merchants in the Montana gold fields, as financiers and devoted citizens of their adopted city.

By stagecoach and muleback Edward surveyed the western telegraph route and was a prime builder for the line completed in 1861. The Creightons provided poles, surveyed, built, rebuilt or raised and collected subscriptions for a good portion of the lines extending west from Buffalo, N.Y., to San Francisco.

In 1863 Edward became the initial president of the first national bank opened in Omaha. This civic leader gave freely of his time and substance to assure Omaha's position as eastern terminus of the Union Pacific Railroad. Thus, both major national projects of the last half of the nineteenth century owed much to these pioneers.

Creighton University, a memorial to these men, opened its doors in 1878. It has grown to this complex institution with many academic divisions.

Edward Creighton
Nebraska State Historical Society

John A. Creighton
Nebraska State Historical Society

NEBRASKA
HISTORICAL MARKER

CAPITOL HILL

This site on Capitol Hill was for a decade the location of Nebraska's second territorial capitol. The building was erected here in 1857 and 1858 and served until the seat of government was removed to Lincoln in 1868.

Acting-Governor Cuming designated Omaha as the Capital of Nebraska Territory by convening the First Territorial Legislature in Omaha on January 16, 1855. It met in a small two story brick building donated by the Council Bluffs and Nebraska Ferry Company and located on Ninth Street between Douglas and Farnam facing the Missouri River. It housed the legislature for the sessions of 1855 and 1857.

The second capitol was a handsome brick building 137 by 93 feet. The supreme court, the library and government offices were on the first floor and the legislature and governor on the second. Corinthian columns planned for the building were removed as unsafe after several had collapsed.

In 1869 the Capitol building and grounds were presented by the state to Omaha for use as a school. The building was pronounced unsafe and the first public Omaha High School was erected in its place on Capitol Hill in 1872. The present Central High School building completed in 1912 replaced the earlier building. The central court of the school represents the approximate area of the original capitol.

Acting-Governor Thomas B. Cuming
Nebraska State Historical Society

Located: US 73 - 75 - 20th and Dodge Streets in Omaha.

OFFICIAL STATE MAP: I-29
DOUGLAS COUNTY

27

Nebraska State Historical Society

The Fort Omaha Regiment marches in parade formation in 1893.

OFFICIAL STATE MAP: I-29
DOUGLAS COUNTY

Located: US 73 - 30th and Camden Streets in Omaha at fort entrance.

NEBRASKA HISTORICAL MARKER

FORT OMAHA

A military post was first established here in 1868 and named Sherman Barracks after the famous Civil War general, William Tecumseh Sherman. The post's name was soon changed to Omaha Barracks and, in 1878, to Fort Omaha. In 1879, General George Crook, noted Indian fighter and head (1875-1882, 1886-1888) of the Army's Department of the Platte, occupied a new brick home here which is still standing.

By the late 1880's, the 80-some acres of Fort Omaha had become insufficient for the Army's needs. A larger post, Fort Crook, was established near Bellevue and Fort Omaha was closed in 1896. In 1905, it reopened as an Army Signal Corps training school. Closed in 1913, the fort again reopened in 1916, this time as a training school for the crews of Army observation balloons. About 16,000 men trained here in preparation for service in World War I.

When the Army declared Fort Omaha surplus property in 1947, it became a Naval Reserve Manpower Center. Since then it has served as a recruiting, training, and administrative facility for several branches of the armed forces.

Located: AK-SAR-BEN,
Omaha, Nebraska.

NEBRASKA
HISTORICAL MARKER

OMAHA

Buried here at Ak-Sar-Ben is Omaha, one of the immortals of the American turf. His sire Gallant Fox was the 1930 winner of the Triple Crown, and Omaha succeeded him to this title in 1935. To win the Triple Crown a three-year-old must win the Kentucky Derby, Preakness, and Belmont Stakes. They are the only father-son combination to achieve this honor.

Omaha was foaled March 24, 1932, at Clairborne Breeding Farm in Paris, Kentucky. He was owned by William G. Woodward's famed Belair Stud. The chestnut colt was out of Flambino by Wrack, standing 16.3 hands and weighing 1,300 pounds in his prime. He was trained by "Sunny Jim" Fitzsimmons and ridden in his great American races by William "Smokey" Saunders. As a four-year-old Omaha was shipped to England where he won the Victor Wild Stakes and the Queen's Plate.

Omaha was retired to stud after his fourth season. In 1950 he was brought to Nebraska by breeders interested in improving Nebraska thoroughbreds. He was taken to the Grove Porter Farm near Nebraska City where he lived until his death on April 24, 1959. He was buried here by special invitation from Ak-Sar-Ben in honor of the great place he had earned in the annals of American racing. Betti Richard, an internationally known sculptor, fashioned the lifelike bronze figure of Omaha which marks the grave.

NEBRASKA
HISTORICAL MARKER

1871 FILLMORE COUNTY 1971

The first homesteads were filed in 1866 by William O. Bussard and William B. Whitaker along the West Fork of the Blue River. Mrs. E. A. Whitaker, the first white woman, came in 1867. The first white children, Emma Whitaker Hall, and Arthur Dixon were born in 1869. Fillmore City was the first town platted in 1870. Other settlers soon followed, and on April 21, 1871 an election was held for officers to organize a new county, named for President Millard Fillmore. The county seat was named for Geneva, Illinois, the former home of Nathaniel McCalla in whose dugout the election was held.

The completion of the Burlington & Missouri River Railroad across the county in 1871, resulted in large numbers of settlers taking up the land and the towns of Exeter, Fairmont and Grafton were platted. Other towns now in the county are Furress, Milligan, Ohiowa, Shickley and Strang.

The early pioneers came from varied origins, Anglo-Saxon, Bohemian, German, and Swedish. Indians were not a major threat to the settlers but blizzards, grasshoppers, prairie fires and droughts were major hazards. HONOUR TO PIONEERS WHO BROKE THE SOD THAT MEN TO COME MIGHT LIVE.

OFFICIAL STATE MAP: M-24
FILLMORE COUNTY

Located: US 81 - courthouse lawn in Geneva.

Main Street, Fairmont

Nebraska State Historical Society

Located: US 136 - Court-
house square at Franklin.

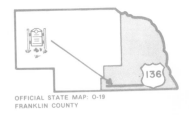

OFFICIAL STATE MAP: O-19
FRANKLIN COUNTY

NEBRASKA
HISTORICAL MARKER

FRANKLIN COUNTY

Present Franklin County was formerly a part of the buffalo hunting range of the Pawnee Indians, whose villages were at one time located further down the valley of the Republican River. Cheyenne and Sioux hunting parties also frequented the area prior to 1869, when General Carr's Republican River Expedition cleared the valley of hostiles, opening the region to white settlement.

In September 1870, the Thompson Colony founded Riverton in the eastern part of the county, and the Republican Land and Claim Association or Knight Colony arrived on November 25th, to found the town of Franklin. In the Spring of 1871, a small Negro colony attempted to found a settlement, but their lack of finances forced its abandonment.

By proclamation of Governor Butler, the county was organized on March 3, 1871, with Franklin as the county seat. Nearby Bloomington, site of the U.S. Land Office for the region, won the county seat in 1874, where it remained until 1920. With the arrival of the railroad in 1879, this fertile country was soon settled by homesteaders, many of whose descendants still reside here. Founded during years of depression and natural disaster, Franklin County has a proud heritage.

Buffalo grazed on Nebraska's rolling prairie.

Nebraska State Historical Society

31

Located: US 77 - 1 mile north of Beatrice, Beatrice Airport.

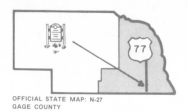

OFFICIAL STATE MAP: N-27
GAGE COUNTY

NEBRASKA
HISTORICAL MARKER

HOMESTEAD MOVEMENT

Abraham Lincoln was called the Great Emancipator because his proclamation of 1862 gave freedom to the slaves. In that same year, he signed another extremely important document that gave land to free men. No single act had more effect on the Middle West and Great Plains than the Homestead Act of May 20, 1862. It brought tens of thousands of land-hungry settlers to the region that was to become the nation's breadbasket.

Millions of acres from the public domain became available. Under this law heads of families had only to pay a small filing fee and live upon and cultivate their 160 acres for five years. For some the rigors of frontier life were too great, but many others replaced the prairie grasses with grain, and built homes, often of sod, on land of their own.

The Homestead National Monument of America, a part of our National Park System, is located on the Daniel Freeman homestead seven miles west of this site. It commemorates this act and the policies of government that played a major role in the settlement of the West.

Mr. and Mrs. Daniel Freeman with their children   Nebraska State Historical Society

Homestead National
Monument of America

NATIONAL MONUMENT

Free Land was the constant cry of frontiersmen who, during the first six decades of America's history, wanted the Federal Government to donate land to settlers. The response came on May 20, 1862, when President Abraham Lincoln signed the Homestead Act, destined to be one of the most important measures enacted in the history of this country. Western Congressmen were early advocates of the basic principle of the Homestead Act: free land to settlers. The earliest important supporter was Senator Thomas Hart Benton of Missouri. Andrew Johnson of Tennessee (first as a Representative and later as a Senator), Representative Galusha Grow of Pennsylvania and Horace Greeley, editor of the **New York Tribune**, were among the champions of the cause.

Nonsectional both in origin and during its early history, the homestead movement attracted diverse support as it gained force and popularity. First minor, and later major, political parties included it in their platforms.

Later the newly formed Republican Party urged passage of a homestead act. Antislavery groups, who opposed extension of slavery into the territories, supported the principle of free land. Thus was homesteading entangled in the controversies leading to the Civil War.

Between 1840 and 1860, the movement for a homestead law slowly crystallized. At first it received some support from the southeastern States. As the alliance between the agrarian West and the industrial East became stronger, however, homestead proposals encountered increasing opposition from the slave States. Several bills were seriously considered in Congress, but were killed by Southern opposition.

Located: Nebraska 4 - 4½ miles northwest of Beatrice.

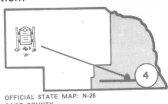

OFFICIAL STATE MAP: N-26
GAGE COUNTY

As the natural prairie covering, Blue Stem Grass was the road, pillow and cattle fodder for the westward-bound pioneers of the 1800s.

National Park Service

BLUE STEM
(ANDROPOGON – GERARDI)
NATIVE PRAIRIE GRASS

LAND FOR THE LANDLESS

On May 6, after many amendments, a homestead bill passed the Senate by a vote of 33 to 7. On May 20, President Lincoln signed the Homestead Act into law.

The act made it possible for settlers to acquire farms of 160 acres free of all charges, except for a minor filing fee. To become full owner, a settler had to live on the land and cultivate it for 5 years. Later acts made land even easier to get, especially for veterans of the Army and the Navy.

The end of the Civil War released thousands of men to seek a livelihood in a country disrupted by 4 years of upheaval. Many took advantage of the free public lands offered by the Homestead Act. A free farm, added to the other opportunities held forth by a democratic nation, lured many Europeans to seek new homes in America.

Largely because the supply of public land suitable for homesteading was exhausted, remaining public lands were withdrawn from homesteading in 1935.

From existing evidence it is impossible to determine who filed the first claim, since application papers were not stamped with the minute and hour of filing, only the date. Daniel Freeman's homestead, on which the monument is located, was filed at the Brownville, Nebr., Patent Office as Entry No. 1 (dated January 1, 1863), Final Certificate No. 1 and Patent No. 1—all first entries for Brownville but not for the United States. Freeman, in common with Mahlon Gore, a printer of Vermillion, S. Dak., claimed that he filed his application for a homestead in the early hours of January 1, 1863, when the Homestead Act went into effect. Another claimant, William Young, asserted years later that his entry became effective immediately after midnight, December 31, because he filed, and had accepted, his claim at Nebraska City, Nebr., on December 26, 1862. Other claimants may also have filed at other land offices in the first hours of 1863.

Daniel Freeman and his wife, Agnes Suiter Freeman, are buried near the monument's eastern boundary, the highest point on the homestead. From the grave sites, marked by a granite stone, you can see the full panorama of the quarter section that Freeman homesteaded.

Built on another homestead 14 miles away in 1867, the Palmer-Epard Cabin is a one-room brick and log structure that at one time housed a family of ten.

National Park Service

NATIONAL MONUMENT

Establishing the Monument

During the early 1930's, a movement was launched to set aside Daniel Freeman's land as a memorial to the homestead movement. The efforts of Senator George W. Norris, the Beatrice Chamber of Commerce, and local citizens were rewarded in 1936 when Congress authorized establishment of the monument ''as a proper memorial emblematical of the hardships . . . through which the early settlers passed in the settlement . . . of the great West.''

Homestead National Monument, a T-shaped quarter section of prairie and woodland near Beatrice, Nebr., is on the site of the claim of Daniel Freeman, one of the first applicants to file under the Homestead Act. The monument, commemorating the influence of the ''homestead movement'' on American history, is a memorial to the hardy pioneers who braved the rigors and scourges of the windswept prairies to build their homes and our Nation.

The visitor center is near the monument entrance. On exhibit are historic objects of pioneer days and graphic accounts of life during settlement of the public domain. National Park Service personnel will help you become better acquainted with the monument and its history.

These persons are recreating two steps in the process of making lye soap. The man is stomping ashes in a rack to help water filter through to hasten the lye process. The woman is stirring the thickening lye soap. Both are wearing common homesteader everyday clothes.

National Park Service

National Park Service

NATIONAL
MONUMENT

The Palmer-Epard homestead cabin, erected in 1867 in a neighboring township and moved here in 1950, is on display. Its furnishings and tools, which were used by pioneers' in eastern Nebraska, suggest the pattern of life followed by homesteaders on the tall grass prairie.

A 1-mile self-guiding trail, which begins at the visitor center, leads to the homestead cabin exhibit, the site of the original Freeman Cabin, and the sites of later Freeman buildings, including the brick house of 1876. You can take side trips to the Freeman graves at the eastern boundary of the area and to the Squatters Cabin site near Cub Creek. Special guide service for large groups can be arranged in advance with the superintendent.

This is a recreated scene of a living history demonstration. The young woman is churning butter using the same tools as the homesteaders did in Nebraska in the 1800s.

National Park Service

Nebraska State Historical Society
Nathaniel Martin holding the arrows
that pierced both he and his brother.

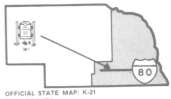

OFFICIAL STATE MAP: K-21
HALL COUNTY

Located: I-80 West - Alda
Rest Area.

NEBRASKA
HISTORICAL MARKER

MARTIN BROTHERS

The general Indian uprising of 1864 centering in the Platte Valley caused great loss of life and property among the early settlers. The area of one of the most dramatic events associated with this outbreak is marked with a stone monument three miles south of here.

There, on a day in August, 1864, George Martin, an ex-English jockey who had come to Hall County in 1862, and his two young sons, Nat and Robert, were loading hay in a field near their homestead. Suddenly they were attacked by a small band of Sioux Indians. While the father attempted to ward off the attackers from the wagon with his repeating rifle, the boys jumped on their mare and, riding double, started for home.

Pursued by the Sioux, the fleeing pony and her riders became targets for numerous arrows, one of which passed through Nat's body and lodged in Robert's back. Thus pinned together by a single arrow, the boys tumbled from their horse. The Indians, evidently believing that the boys were nearly dead, rode away without scalping them. Robert never recovered fully from his back injury, and although Nat nearly died of his wounds he lived to tell this story to his grandchildren.

Martin Ranch as it appeared in 1866

Nebraska State Historical Society

THE MORMON TRAIL

Religious freedom, an American ideal, has on occasion been denied certain sects because of prejudice. Mormons were once persecuted and forced from their homes. The north bank of the Platte River served as the exodus route for thousands of members of the Church of Jesus Christ of Latter-day Saints (Mormons). Driven from Nauvoo, Illinois, Mormon leader Brigham Young led the first migration up this valley in 1847 to found the proposed state of Deseret, now Utah.

During the following two decades, thousands more gathered at Winter Quarters on the west bank of the Missouri River near present Florence, Nebraska, before beginning the trek across the plains and mountains to their land of Milk and Honey. The journey called for strength and courage, as well as faith, for tragedy often stalked their wagons and handcarts, turning this valley into a Mormon "trail of tears." Hundreds of pioneers lie buried along this trail, most in unmarked graves.

After 1860 the overland trail along the south bank of the river was lined with road ranches and stage stations, but the Mormon Trail had few such conveniences, and the pioneer settlements here in Hall County were almost the last vestiges of civilization until the travelers reached Utah.

Brigham Young at age 52

Nebraska State Historical Society

Located: Stuhr Museum in Grand Island.

OFFICIAL STATE MAP: K-21
HALL COUNTY

Located: US 281 - Stolley Park Road west of South Locust Street at Grand Island.

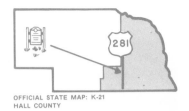

OFFICIAL STATE MAP: K-21
HALL COUNTY

NEBRASKA
HISTORICAL MARKER

LA GRANDE ISLE

Grand Island, in the Platte River, has given its name to the city of Grand Island. The island was formed by a narrow channel branching off the Platte River approximately 28 miles upstream from the present city of Grand Island and rejoining the main river about 12 miles downstream from the city.

The name "Grand Island" came from the French name "La Grande Isle", meaning the large or great island. The island probably was discovered and named by French fur traders in the late 1700's. Grand Island or Grand Isle was a well-known landmark for fur traders by 1810. The name Grand Isle appears on a French map published in 1821 and on American maps published in 1822 and 1823.

Both the Long and Fremont exploring expeditions of 1820 and 1842 took note of the size of Grand Island and west-bound travelers of the 1830's often mentioned the island as the most conspicuous feature of the Central Platte Valley.

Grand Island was ceded to the United States Government by the Pawnee Indians in 1848. The modern history of the island begins with the arrival of the first permanent settlers on July 5, 1857.

Nebraska State Historical Society

Grand Island

39

Nebraska State Historical Society

Mr. and Mrs. William Stolley depicted in painting completed in 1856.

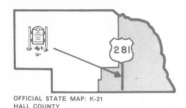

OFFICIAL STATE MAP: K-21
HALL COUNTY

Located: US 281 - in front of stadium on Fonner Park Road 7 blocks east of Locust Street at Grand Island.

NEBRASKA
HISTORICAL MARKER

THE O.K. STORE

The first settlers of Hall County, Nebraska, nearly all of whom were German immigrants, arrived on July 5, 1857. They platted Grand Island City and established farms. The O.K. Store of Henry A. Koenig and Fred Wiebe, located near the Mormon Trail, was opened near this site in 1862. It was the first store in the settlement and it also served as the first telegraph station.

During the Indian uprising of 1864 and 1865 many Platte Valley settlers fled but the Grand Island settlers remained. They fortified the O.K. Store with a sod stockade which sheltered 68 men and 100 women. To give shelter to 35 more persons, William Stolley built "Fort Independence" about two miles west.

On August 22, 1865, General S. R. Curtis and his troops visited "Fort O.K." Impressed by the settlers' preparations for defense Curtis left a six-pounder cannon, which is still preserved in Hall County. Because of the fortifications "Fort O.K." and Grand Island escaped Indian attacks.

In 1858, a short distance northeast of this marker, the first post office for Grand Island was located in John D. Schuller's cabin, which now stands on the county museum grounds.

Located: US 30 - Pioneer Park at Grand Island.

Nebraska State Historical Society

General Grenville M. Dodge was a railroad builder of the 1850s.

NEBRASKA HISTORICAL MARKER

PIONEER PARK

Pioneer Park, site of the first Hall County Courthouse, honors the courageous settlers who peacefully inhabited this area in 1857 when only Pawnee lived here. In 1866 the Union Pacific reached Grand Island and in 1868 the railroad donated Block 19 for the construction of county buildings. Three years later the county commissioners requested that General Grenville M. Dodge, agent and trustee of the railroad, exchange the property for Block 84 where this park is located.

Special elections were held in 1872, where in bonds totalling $20,000 were issued for construction. A two story courthouse with a clock tower was completed June 28, 1873 at a cost of $16,500. In 1901 a special election voted bonds for a new courthouse and other county buildings. When the new structure was completed in 1905, the original courthouse was razed.

Four elections were held from 1902 to 1905 to authorize the sale of this block, but dedicated work by the Women's Park Association maintained this site as a memorial to Hall County pioneers. In 1964 action was brought to construct a new postoffice on this land and a 1970 election was held to locate a new library here, but the park was preserved on both occasions.

NEBRASKA
HISTORICAL   MARKER

DEEP WELL IRRIGATION

During the 1930's, Nebraska suffered one of the most serious droughts in its recorded history. In all parts of Nebraska rainfall was far below normal. In 1936, corn yielded only 1/10 as much per acre as it had during the years 1923-1932. The dry powdered soil began to blow, and as dust storms obscured the sun, parts of Nebraska and the Great Plains became "the Dust Bowl." Between 1930 and 1940, the state declined in population because of the unfavorable agricultural conditions.

This experience resulted in the increased use of deep-well irrigation. Nebraska is fortunate in having the largest supply of groundwater in the central part of the United States. Hamilton County lies somewhat east of the center of the irrigation well area in Nebraska. A 225 foot deep well, sunk in the county by F. E. Edgerton in 1931, remains one of the deepest in the area. It is not uncommon for irrigated land to produce more than twice the crop raised on non-irrigated land. Irrigation is an important factor in the occupation of Nebraska by an agricultural population.

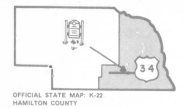

OFFICIAL STATE MAP: K-22
HAMILTON COUNTY

Located: US 34 - northern entrance of Aurora City Park.

A dust storm struck the Naponee area on March 26, 1935. _{Nebraska State Historical Society}

Located: US 183 and Nebraska 4 - 2 miles west of Ragan.

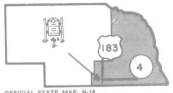

OFFICIAL STATE MAP: N-18
HARLAN COUNTY

NEBRASKA
HISTORICAL MARKER

PIONEER CROSSING

Crossing streams and rivers, in a region where roads were but trails and bridges were unknown, was a major problem to emigrants traveling by team and wagon. To find or construct a ford, such as Wilson's or Pioneer Crossing, was always necessary.

At an unknown date, a grading was cut in the steep banks of Turkey Creek near here so that wagons could cross from one side to the other with relative ease. Logs were bound together with wire and tied to large trees on both banks, forming a bridge over which the wagons could be driven. Occasionally, however, high water would force the pioneers to camp on the banks of Turkey Creek until the water subsided.

The area was first settled in the 1870's. Andrew Wilson, upon whose land the ford was located and from whom it received its name, received his final homestead patent for this land in 1884. During the 1880's, the name of the ford gradually changed from Wilson's to Pioneer Crossing, as most of those using it were westward bound pioneers. A steel bridge was built across Turkey Creek at this site in 1908.

National Park Service

Fording the Platte River

43

Rock Creek
State Historical Park

(under construction)
One of the Pony Express stations used to advance the mails through Nebraska will be rebuilt at the developing Rock Creek State Historical Park east of Fairbury. "Wild Bill" Hickock started his career as a bad man at Rock Creek when he killed the unpaid former owner of a relay station. Very striking samples of Oregon Trail ruts may still be seen in the park.

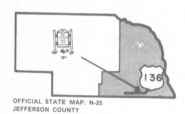

OFFICIAL STATE MAP: N-25
JEFFERSON COUNTY

Located: US 136 - park east of Fairbury. (State Park under construction.)

THE
PONY EXPRESS
TRAIL
1860 - 1861

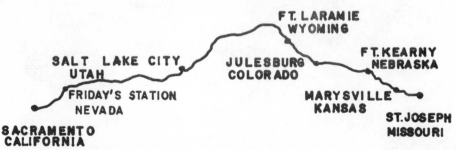

STATE HISTORICAL PARK

Nebraska State Historical Society David Colbert McCanles

On July 12, 1861, near the Rock Creek Station Post Office Wild Bill Hickok shot and killed David C. McCanles.

Nebraska Game and Parks Commission

James Butler Hickok, alias Wild Bill, started his legend at the wild pony express station, Rock Creek.

Nebraska State Historical Society

STATE
HISTORICAL
PARK

These men founded, owned and operated the short-lived Pony Express Line.

The hey-day of the Pony Express lasted less than a year. But during that time the 120 riders rode 650,000 miles. The Pony Express Line had only one rider killed by Indians, one schedule run not completed and one mail lost.

Nebraska State Historical Society
Cornelius Jansen, Sr.

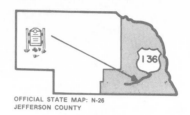

OFFICIAL STATE MAP: N-26
JEFFERSON COUNTY

Located: US 136 - south-western edge of Jansen.

NEBRASKA
HISTORICAL MARKER

JANSEN

In 1874-1875, this area was settled by a group of Mennonites led by Cornelius and Peter Jansen. Many of these settlers were descendants of Dutch emigrants who left Holland in the 16th Century and founded a colony in Russia. Coming to Jefferson County, the Mennonites purchased some 25,000 acres of land from the Burlington and Missouri Railroad.

The Mennonites had developed a unique pattern of community organization which they retained when they came to Nebraska. Their Community as a whole was composed of several so-called "line villages," each of which contained a number of dwellings located close together along both sides of a section line or road. About 1900, one such village, "Russian Lane," reportedly contained some 42 houses, churches and schools along both sides of a 4½ mile road.

Jansen was named for Peter Jansen on whose land the town was platted in 1886. His nearby ranch was noted for its large sheep-raising operation. Peter Jansen was elected to the Nebraska Legislature in 1898 and 1910, and remained active in political affairs until his death in 1923. Today the Jansen community continues to preserve the spirit of its dedicated pioneers.

Nebraska State Historical Society

Peter Jansen mounted on his favorite horse.

NEBRASKA
HISTORICAL MARKER

THE SMITH LIMEKILN AND LIMESTONE HOUSE

The availability of suitable building material was of great importance to Nebraska's pioneer settlers. Here in Jefferson County, native limestone was used for building and the stone was burned in kilns to produce lime for mortar and whitewash. The U.S. Army reportedly operated the first kiln in this area during the 1848 construction of Fort Kearny on the Platte. During the 1870's and 1880's, the limestone industry flourished in Jefferson County and numerous kilns and quarries were located near here.

The limekiln which survives on this site was built in 1874 by Woral C. Smith who had settled in the county the previous year. Much of the limestone from Smith's quarries was used locally, but after the St. Joseph and Denver City Railroad built a siding to the kiln, limestone products were shipped throughout the region. In 1876, Smith constructed the nearby house with limestone from his quarries.

Today, commercial limestone production continues in several areas of Nebraska. Although the old limekilns have largely disappeared, the Smith kiln and limestone house remain as examples of this important pioneer industry.

Limestone House

Nebraska State Historical Society

Located: US 136 - gravel road east of bridge west of Fairbury, 4 miles northwest on River Road to park.

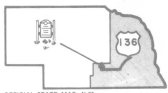

OFFICIAL STATE MAP: N-25
JEFFERSON COUNTY

STATE
HISTORICAL
PARK

Located: Nebraska 10 - 9 miles north of Minden, State Spur 50-A.

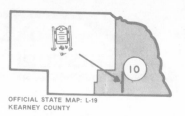

OFFICIAL STATE MAP: L-19
KEARNEY COUNTY

Nebraska State Historical Society

Brevet Major General Daniel P. Woodbury

Fort Kearny State Historical Park

In the spring of 1848, Lieutenant Daniel P. Woodbury began construction on Fort Kearny at this site. Woodbury called the new post Fort Childs. However, a general order for the War Department officially named it Fort Kearny in honor of Colonel Stephen Watts Kearny.

The first Fort Kearny had been established by Colonel Kearny himself on Table Creek in what is now Nebraska City, Nebraska. This location proved to be too far east to provide protection for emigrants on the Oregon Trail and was ordered relocated. Congress had ordered a chain of forts and blockhouses constructed for the protection of travelers after the emigration to the Oregon Territory began to increase considerably after 1842.

The California Gold Rush also increased travel on the Trail. According to an 1849 War Department report, 30,000 people passed through Fort Kearny during an 18-month period, bound for California, Oregon, and Salt Lake.

Overland Stages carrying mail and passengers, prospectors and miners bound for the gold diggings, emigrants lured by free land in Oregon; and the huge freighting caravans all contributed to making Fort Kearny a bustling center of activity. The post continued to expand in size and

importance. The Pony Express had a ''home'' station here which was later replaced by a telegraph office. Fort Kearny indeed was an important factor in the westward expansion of our nation.

The period following the Civil War saw the Fort's peak development. As the scene of the Indian Wars shifted to the west and north, Fort Kearny became less and less essential to the military. The last function of any importance was to provide protection for the crews constructing the Union Pacific Railroad. In 1871, Fort Kearny was discontinued as a military post.

After abandonment, the buildings were torn down and the fort reservations opened for homesteading. The earthworks of the fortifications and the large cottonwoods around the parade grounds were all that remained.

In 1928, the Fort Kearny Memorial Association was formed and purchased the 40 acres where the majority of the buildings stood. The State of Nebraska accepted title to the land in 1929. Then, the 1959 Legislature enacted a new law classifying state-owned areas and provided funds for their development. Fort Kearny was classified as a state historical park, and development was started in 1960.

Archeological exploration of the area to locate building sites and other features was carried out by the Nebraska State Historical Society on a contract with the Game and Parks Commission. The park is developed to give the visitor an insight into the conditions and events contemporary with the settlement of the American West.

Nebraska Game and Parks Commission

Fort Kearny seen from the northeast in 1870.

STATE HISTORICAL PARK

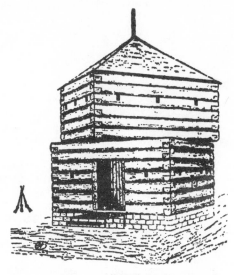

Nebraska State Historical Society

This military block house at Fort Kearny was torn down in 1889.

These are the uniforms of type worn at Fort Kearny.

Nebraska State Historical Society

STATE HISTORICAL PARK

Nebraska Game and Parks Commission
Fort Kearny's restored blacksmith shop

Fort Kearny, near the present town of Kearney, was established in 1848 to offer protection for the pioneers during their westward push through Indian country. Today the old fort is being restored by the Game and Parks Commission as a historical park.

Nebraska Game and Parks Commission

Nebraska State Historical Society

Dobytown in 1863 consisted of Piper & Robertson's store; boarding house; saloon and restaurant.

OFFICIAL STATE MAP: L-19
KEARNEY COUNTY

Located: US 30 - southeast of Kearney and west of Nebraska 44 on State Spur 50-A.

NEBRASKA
HISTORICAL MARKER

DOBYTOWN

Following the 1848 establishment of Fort Kearny three miles east of here and the later expansion of overland commerce and emigration, the small commercial center of Kearney City was established here in 1859. The town's more common name, Dobytown, was derived from the resemblance of its twelve to fifteen earthern buildings to adobe structures.

Dobytown itself developed in response to the thousands of soldiers, freighters and travelers whose "needs" could not be met within the fort. Gambling, liquor and disreputable men and women were its principal attractions. One of the town's most famous visitors, General William Tecumseh Sherman described the horrible whiskey he was served here as "tanglefoot." However, in addition to its notorious functions, Dobytown also served as the major outfitting point west of the Missouri River, the center of frontier transportation from 1860 to 1866, a Pony Express station and the first county seat of Kearney County.

The completion of the Union Pacific Railroad in 1869 reduced the flow of travel by the fort until finally in 1871 it was abandoned, sounding the death knell of Dobytown, a pioneer frontier town.

Located: US 34 - 6 - northeast of Minden at townsite.

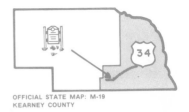

OFFICIAL STATE MAP: M-19
KEARNEY COUNTY

NEBRASKA
HISTORICAL MARKER

1872 LOWELL 1972

The Boom Town played an important role in the West, and few Nebraska towns had such a boom history as Lowell. It was selected as a townsite by the Burlington & Missouri River Railroad in 1871, and its first businesses were soon established.

Lowell, first incorporated town in Kearney County, was chosen county seat at the re-organization election of June 17, 1872. The railroad arrived on July 8th, and for a short time it was end-of-track, becoming a major shipping point for central Nebraska. Also in July, it was selected as the site for the U.S. Land Office for the Republican Valley, and its streets were crowded with homesteaders. It was a temporary shipping point for herds of cattle trailed north from Texas. The courthouse and land office stood near here.

Lowell's decline began as early as 1873, when the railroad built on to Kearney, making it the regional trading center, and a bridge built across the Platte at Kearney in 1874 continued the drop in business. The removal of the land office in 1874 added to the decline of Lowell. When the county seat was removed in 1878, a quiet village replaced the boom town. The school closed in 1963.

PONCA INDIANS

This is the homeland of the Ponca Indians who have lived in this area since earliest recorded history. In 1868, the federal government signed the Treaty of Fort Laramie which transferred the land to the Sioux without the permission of the Ponca. Treaties made with the government in 1858 had guaranteed their land to them. The Ponca were forcibly removed to Indian Territory in 1877. Unable to adjust to the climate of the South, many became ill and died. Among these was the son of Chief Standing Bear.

In January 1879, the chief and his small band left Indian Territory bearing the remains of his son for burial in Nebraska. When troops arrested the small band, white friends came to their aid. As a result of a court decision it was determined that "an Indian is a person within the meaning of the law." This important action did much to provide legal rights for all Indians.

A Nebraska reservation was eventually assigned to the Northern Ponca while many of the Southern Ponca remained in Oklahoma. In 1962, at the request of the Ponca, Congress provided for a termination of the reservation. Today the Ponca can be proud of their fight for justice.

Ponca Chief Standing Bear
Nebraska State Historical Society

Located: Nebraska 14 - 1½ miles south of intersection of 12 and 14 at scenic turnout.

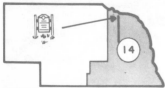

OFFICIAL STATE MAP: C-22
KNOX COUNTY

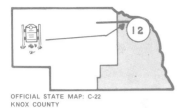

OFFICIAL STATE MAP: C-22
KNOX COUNTY

Located: Nebraska 12 - Ball Park, southern edge of Niobrara.

Gary

Gregory

Kelly

NEBRASKA
HISTORICAL MARKER

THE SAGE BROTHERS

On the night of June 2, 1969, while on maneuvers in the South China Sea off the coast of Vietnam, the Australian aircraft carrier Melbourne was in collision with the destroyer USS Frank E. Evans. The impact cut the Evans in two, the bow section sinking almost immediately. Seventy-four American seamen were lost, including three brothers from Niobrara, Nebraska; Gary, Gregory, and Kelly Sage. The brothers, 22, 21, and 19 years of age respectively, were the sons of Mr. and Mrs. Ernest Sage, and had been stationed together aboard the Evans at their own request. This tragedy was perhaps the greatest single loss suffered by any Nebraska family of the many who have contributed their sons to the service of the Nation.

At memorial services in Niobrara on June 11, 1969, the Governor of Nebraska eulogized the brothers saying that "Every generation of Americans has answered the call to the colors . . . So it was with the Sage brothers who were serving in the finest tradition of the American fighting man. In the truest sense, they gave up their lives that we might continue to enjoy the fruits of freedom . . ."

STATE MUSEUM

Nebraska State Historical Society Museum

FROM THE ATLATL TO THE ATLAS

From the prehistoric Indians who hunted with a throwing device known as an atlatl through the Atlas missile bases recently removed from the state, Nebraska has been the scene of exciting chapters in the history of the West. Highlights of this story are recreated in the galleries of the Nebraska State Historical Society Museum in Lincoln.

In the Indian Gallery, grinding stones, projectile points, and other artifacts trace the development of prehistoric Plains Indians from hunter to farmer. Other items interpret the farming-villager tribes of eastern and central Nebraska. Feathered headdresses, beaded clothing, and painted buffalo robes recreate the flamboyant life of the Sioux, Cheyenne, and Arapaho in western Nebraska.

In the Pioneer Gallery, a cowboy camp and immigrant clothing are two displays illustrating westward expansion. Other exhibits point out the hardships of settling the sod house frontier. Displays featuring Buffalo Bill and Wild Bill Hickok emphasize the drama of the Old West.

Upstairs is a Special Exhibits Gallery featuring period rooms, while in the basement such items as china dolls and hair wreaths are displayed in Collector's Lane.

Located: I-80 - 1500 R Street in Lincoln.

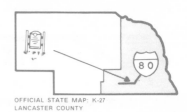

OFFICIAL STATE MAP: K-27
LANCASTER COUNTY

The Nebraska State Historical Society Museum and Administrative Offices

Nebraska State Historical Society

STATE

MUSEUM

LIBRARY

On the second floor of the Society building is an ever-expanding research library of interest to scholars and laymen alike. Both out-of-print and current publications can be found here, as well as thousands of photographs and some of the most extensive genealogical research materials in the area.

ARCHIVES

The State Archives, also on the second floor, serves as a depository for manuscripts, letters, and valuable public records of all kinds. It also maintains an extensive file of current and historical Nebraska newspapers, largely on microfilm.

EDUCATIONAL AIDS

Each year, thousands of school children receive guided tours of the museum, where films and puppet shows increase their knowledge of Nebraska history. Educational leaflets and teachers' packets are also available to schools.

OTHER MUSEUMS

The Society also maintains a branch museum at Fort Robinson, near Crawford, Nebraska; is in charge of the Nebraska Statehood Memorial, the Thomas P. Kennard House at 1627 H Street in Lincoln; and assists in the research for the restored William Jennings Bryan Home at 4900 Sumner in Lincoln.

This is one of the museum's life-size displays on the homesteading settlement of the plains.

Nebraska State Historical Society

Nebraska State Historical Society

One of the audio displays at the Nebraska State Historical Society Museum is about the early days of fur trading with the plains Indians.

MEMBERSHIP

Membership in the Nebraska State Historical Society is open to everyone. All members receive Nebraska History, the Society's quarterly magazine, and the monthly Historical News Letter. Membership also allows individuals to actively participate in Society programs to preserve and interpret Nebraska's history.

Nebraska State Historical Society

The wild romantic days of Texas Longhorn cattle drives to the Nebraska railroad towns are recreated in this life-size museum display using the authentic tools of the cowboys.

An engraving of Salt Basin and Salt Works at Lincoln

Nebraska State Historical Society

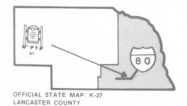

OFFICIAL STATE MAP: K-27
LANCASTER COUNTY

Located: I-80 - 10th and J Streets in Lincoln. Marker is east of building.

NEBRASKA
HISTORICAL MARKER

COUNTY-CITY BUILDING
Lincoln, Lancaster County, Nebraska

On March 6, 1855, Lancaster County was created by act of the Territorial Legislature. Many early settlers came for land, while others were attracted by the commercial possibilities of the nearby Salt Basin. In 1859, a site east of the Salt Basin was selected as the future county seat. Originally known as Lancaster, the town was first settled in 1864 and renamed Lincoln in 1867 when it was designated the state capital.

Lincoln's city government occupied various locations until 1886, when a municipal headquarters building was erected at 10th and Q Streets. The old U.S. Post Office building, constructed in 1874-1879 at 10th and O Streets, served as City Hall from 1907-1969.

In 1888, the County Commissioners accepted a bid of $164,976 for the construction of Lancaster County's first courthouse. Completed in 1890 on a site directly north of this building, the courthouse was razed in 1969.

Through the combined efforts of the City Council and County Commissioners, voter approval was received in 1965 for the construction of a building to house both governments. Designed by two local architectural firms, the County-City Building was completed in 1969 at a cost of five million dollars.

Nebraska State Historical Society
William Jennings Bryan

OFFICIAL STATE MAP: K-27
LANCASTER COUNTY

Located: I-80 - 50th and Sumner Streets by the Bryan Home in Lincoln.

NEBRASKA
HISTORICAL MARKER

FAIRVIEW
Home of William Jennings Bryan

William Jennings Bryan was born in Salem, Illinois in 1860. He moved to Lincoln in 1887, entered into law practice and was elected to Congress in 1890. He won the first of three presidential nominations with his "Cross of Gold" speech at the Democratic National Convention in 1896. Fairview was built in 1901-1902 with the proceeds from his publications. Construction costs were more than $10,000.00.

Bryan visualized Fairview as a new Monticello and accepted the 1908 presidential nomination on the front steps of the home. Woodrow Wilson visited here during the 1912 campaign and a steady parade of political personalities came to consult with "The Great Commoner". Here he collected the mementos of his unsuccessful political campaigns and world tour of 1905.

Fairview was the scene of many lawn parties held by the Bryans for their friends. The surrounding fields were farmed under his watchful eye. Mrs. Bryan's health forced the family to leave Nebraska in 1917 after Bryan had served as President Wilson's Secretary of State. In 1922 Fairview was deeded to the Lincoln Methodist Hospital, now Bryan Memorial Hospital. William Jennings Bryan died in 1925 after the famed Scopes trial and is buried in Arlington National Cemetery.

Nebraska State Historical Society

This crowd gathered near Bryan's home, Fairview, following the notification ceremonies in August, 1908.

Nebraska State Historical Society

Thomas R. Kennard

Nebraska State Historical Society

Nebraska Statehood Memorial Today

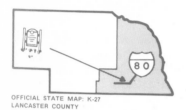

OFFICIAL STATE MAP: K-27
LANCASTER COUNTY

Located: I-80 - 1627 H Street
in front of Kennard House in
Lincoln.

NEBRASKA
HISTORICAL MARKER

NEBRASKA STATEHOOD MEMORIAL

From 1854 to 1867 the seat of territorial and state government was in Omaha. In 1867 the State Legislature appointed a Capital Commission to select a location for the new state capital. Commission members Governor David Butler, Auditor John Gillespie and Secretary of State Thomas P. Kennard on July 29, 1867 selected the present site.

In 1869 John K. Winchell of Chicago designed masonry homes in Lincoln for each of the Commissioners. These showplaces did much to instill confidence in Lincoln's future. Of these three structures, only the Kennard House stands today. It is apparently the oldest house within the original plat of Lincoln and is one of the finest remaining Nebraska examples of Italianate domestic architecture, the leading American style from about 1855 to 1875, Nebraska's pioneer period.

In 1965 the State Legislature designated the structure the "Nebraska Statehood Memorial" and assigned responsibility for the memorial to the Nebraska State Historical Society. Thus the house stands today, a symbol of the confidence early Nebraskans had in their state.

Located: I-80 - 12th Street onto University Campus, northwest of Sheldon Art Gallery in front of Ferguson Hall in Lincoln.

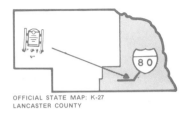

OFFICIAL STATE MAP: K-27
LANCASTER COUNTY

NEBRASKA
HISTORICAL MARKER

THE UNIVERSITY OF NEBRASKA

Chartered as a Land-Grant institution by the first regular session of the State Legislature on February 15, 1869, the University opened its doors to 20 collegiate students and 110 preparatory school pupils on September 7, 1871. Lincoln was then a raw prairie village of about 2,400 people.

University Hall, the original four-story building, stood on this site. Its lumber was hauled by wagon from Nebraska City; its brick made locally. It was finally razed in October, 1948.

Despite financial crises and ideological disputes, the University survived its early years and in 1886 inaugurated the first program of graduate instruction west of the Mississippi. Recognized for its high scholastic standards, the University was accorded membership in the Association of American Universities in 1908.

As a major institution of higher education, the University performed a key role in the early development of the State and continues now as a prime source of further Nebraska progress.

The University of Nebraska, looking up Lincoln's 11th Street, had an enrollment of 67 students in 1876.
Nebraska State Historical Society

65

NEBRASKA
HISTORICAL MARKER

BATTLE CREEK

Near this site, July 12, 1859, Nebraska Territorial Militia and U.S. Army Dragoons, totaling 300 men, under the joint command of General John Milton Thayer and Lieutenant Beverly Holcombe Robertson, prepared to attack a large Pawnee village. Alerted, the Pawnee immediately surrendered. Without bloodshed, the Pawnee War of 1859 was ended.

It had begun July 1st, when messengers arrived at Omaha, the territorial capital, reporting numerous depredations by Pawnee against Elk Horn valley settlers. If the Pawnee were to be punished, immediate action was necessary.

Only the Governor could call out the militia, however, and Governor Samuel Black was a day's journey away. Petitioned by Omaha citizens, Territorial Secretary J. Sterling Morton assumed the responsibility and issued the call. Thayer with forty men left immediately in pursuit. A few days later he was joined by Governor Black with more volunteers and Lieutenant Robertson with Co. K of the 2nd U. S. Dragoons.

Though no battle occurred, the stream where the attack took place became known as Battle Creek, and the nearby town took the same name when founded in 1867.

Governor Samuel W. Black

Nebraska State Historical Society

Located: Intersection of US 275 and Nebraska 121 - 1 mile south of intersection.

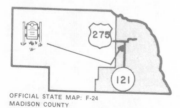

OFFICIAL STATE MAP: F-24
MADISON COUNTY

Located: US 275 - Millstone
Wayside Area Park eastern
edge of Meadow Grove.

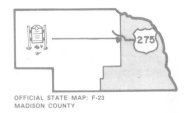

NEBRASKA
HISTORICAL MARKER

MEADOW GROVE

Near here at a point midway between the source of the Elkhorn River and its entry into the Platte, is the town of Meadow Grove. The Elkhorn Valley has long been an important passageway for travelers and settlers. In 1739, the Mallet brothers made the first recorded journey through this region. James Mackay, employed by the Spanish, came through part of the Elkhorn Valley in 1796. These early explorers named the river **Come de Cerf** French for "Elk's Horn."

The Elkhorn attracted settlers of varied origins, many from settlements to the east. In 1879, the Fremont, Elkhorn & Missouri Valley Railroad extended its track through this area.

One of the first signs of the establishment of permanent settlement in any region was the construction of a gristmill. P. V. Lewis, who came to Nebraska in 1869, constructed a mill on Buffalo Creek near here in 1883, using millstones imported from France. Farmers brought grain to the mill from miles around, making it a place for meeting friends as well as milling grain. Lewis later platted the town of Meadow Grove.

This marker erected in memory of all Elkhorn Valley pioneers.

Nebraska State Historical Society

Wagon bridge over the Elkhorn

67

LONE TREE

Lone Tree, a giant, solitary cottonwood, was a noted Platte River Landmark as early as 1833. Standing on the north side of the river some three miles southwest of present Central City, the tree was visible at great distances. Several travelers estimated they could see it twenty miles away. The tree was especially prominent since timber was rare on the Nebraska prairies except in stream valleys, where it received protection from prairie fires.

The Mormon Trail passed by Lone Tree, as did the Omaha-Fort Kearny stage route. The tree also gave its name to a stage station and a town, later renamed Central City. Ten to twelve feet in circumference, the tree's total height was about fifty feet; its lowest branches were about twenty feet above the ground.

Passing travelers often camped beneath Lone Tree and carved their initials on its trunk. This probably hastened its end, for the tree was dead by 1863. A severe storm in 1865 brought it to the earth. In 1911 residents of Merrick County erected a stone in the shape of a tree trunk on the site once occupied by Lone Tree.

Lone Tree Monument

Nebraska State Historical Society

Located: US 30 - 1 mile west of Central City at roadside park.

OFFICIAL STATE MAP: J-22
MERRICK COUNTY

Nebraska State Historical Society

The Great Mormon Caravan crossed the Nebraska prairie via the Oregon-California Trail in 1849.

Located: US 30 and Nebraska 92 - at Mormon Trail Wayside Park northeast of Central City.

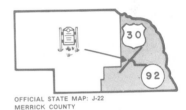

OFFICIAL STATE MAP: J-22
MERRICK COUNTY

NEBRASKA HISTORICAL MARKER

THE MORMON TRAIL

For thousands of Mormons, the great pioneer trail along the north bank of the Platte which paralleled the river about a mile south of here was an avenue of escape from persecution and a roadway to a new life.

Brigham Young led the first mass migration over the Mormon Trail to the Great Salt Lake in 1847. The north bank of the Platte was chosen to avoid contact with the travelers on the heavily-used Oregon Trail that follows the south bank of the river from near Kearney westward. Among the expeditions which followed, were several so poor that pioneers walked and pulled handcarts.

The trail became one of the great roadways to the west, used by Mormons, military expeditions, gold seekers and settlers.

The completion of the Union Pacific Railroad in 1869 ended extensive use of the trail as the railroad tracks followed essentially this same route. Today, the Lincoln Highway (Highway 30) follows this great roadway to the west.

Nebraska State Historical Society

The transportation of supplies to the Mormons already settled at Salt Lake was done by the Conestoga Wagon pulled by oxen.

Located: Nebraska 39 - city park at southern edge of Genoa.

OFFICIAL STATE MAP: H-23
NANCE COUNTY

NEBRASKA
HISTORICAL MARKER

GENOA: 1857-1859

Genoa, named by the Mormon Pioneers, was among several temporary settlements established by the Church of the Latter Day Saints in 1857, along the 1000-mile trail from Florence, Nebraska to Salt Lake City. These settlements were to serve as way-stations for the Brigham Young Express and Carrying Company, which had the government mail contract to Salt Lake City, and as rest and supply stops for Saints traveling across the plains.

Mormons from St. Louis, Florence, and Alton, Illinois were called to establish the Genoa settlement in the spring of 1857, and the Colony arrived here on May 16. During the first year, 100 families settled at Genoa and began to fence the land and plant crops under the direction of Brother Allen, Mission president. A steam powered mill was constructed and log, frame, and sod structures were erected to house the settlers and their livestock.

In the fall of 1859, the Mormon Colony was forced to abandon Genoa when the settlement became part of the newly created Pawnee Indian Reservation. Genoa served as the Pawnee Indian Agency until 1876, when the Pawnee were removed to the Indian Territory and the reservation lands offered for sale.

Nebraska State Historical Society

Band of Pawnee Indians

Located: Nebraska 39
southern edge of Genoa.

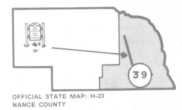

OFFICIAL STATE MAP: H-23
NANCE COUNTY

NEBRASKA
HISTORICAL MARKER

PAWNEE

This was Pawnee Country, the last Nebraska home of an Indian Confederacy which once numbered more than 10,000, consisting of four tribes -- Skidi, Grand, Republican and Tapage. Their domain covered a large part of Central Nebraska where they lived in permanent earth-lodge villages and developed an elaborate religious and social organization. The Pawnee grew corn, made pottery and many flint tools and weapons. They depended on buffalo for their meat and hides, and each year carried on extended hunts along the Platte and Republican rivers where they conflicted with their enemies the Sioux and other Plains Indians.

In 1857 they ceded their remaining lands, with the exception of what is now Nance County and established their villages at this site under their famous Chief, Petalesharo. Nearly always friendly to the Whites, the Pawnee furnished scouts commanded by Major Frank North, which were a colorful and effective fighting force in the Indian wars of 1864-1877.

Under continued harassment by nomadic tribes and demoralized by association with the Whites, the Pawnee dwindled in numbers and prestige. In 1873 they suffered major losses in battle with the Sioux at Massacre Canyon near present day Trenton. In 1874-1875 they left their ancestral Nebraska home for a reservation in Oklahoma.

Nebraska State Historical Society

Persecuted in Illinois, several thousand Mormons made the 1300 mile trek to Salt Lake, Utah, via handmade two wheeled carts.

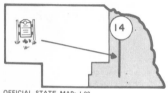

OFFICIAL STATE MAP: I-23
NANCE COUNTY

Located: Nebraska 14 - 2½ miles southwest of Fullerton.

NEBRASKA
HISTORICAL MARKER

MORMON PIONEER CAMPSITE

In the early spring of 1847, several hundred Mormon pioneers camped here on their historic trek to the Valley of the Great Salt Lake. Driven from their homes in Illinois and Missouri, more than 3,000 of the oppressed people had wintered near the present site of Omaha, housed in log cabins, sod houses and dugouts, preparing for the journey to their new Zion in the Rocky Mountains.

The first company of pioneers, led by Brigham Young, left Winter Quarters on April 14 with 143 men, three women and two children traveling in 73 wagons. They arrived in what is now Salt Lake City on July 24, 1847. Several other companies took the trail in the months and years that followed, traveling the same route, and many of them camping at or near this spot.

Between 1855 and 1860 several thousand made the 1300-mile journey on foot, pulling their worldly possessions in handmade two-wheeled carts. The dramatic and ofttimes tragic story of these Handcart Pioneers is one of the epics of American history. Overpowered by summer heat or caught in the cold of prairie blizzards, hundreds of them lie buried in unmarked graves along the trail.

NEBRASKA
HISTORICAL MARKER

BROWNVILLE

On August 29, 1854, shortly after the Kansas-Nebraska Act had opened the territory west of the Missouri River to Permanent settlement, Richard Brown arrived on the site of the town which was to bear his name. Other settlers soon followed.

Brownville quickly became one of the leading towns and cultural centers in the new territory. Located on the river, it became a transfer point for westbound wagon caravans. Here Daniel Freeman filed his homestead claim, recognized as the first in the nation. Brownville was also the site of the first telegraph office in Nebraska.

In 1872, both party candidates for governor were from Brownville. Robert W. Furnas, the Republican, won. Furnas had come to Brownville in 1856 and established one of the state's first newspapers, the **Nebraska Advertiser**. T. W. Tipton, another Brownville resident, served in the U.S. Senate from 1867 to 1875.

Desirous of attracting a railroad, the town approved a huge bond issue in the late 1860's. The contracting company built only ten miles of track. Deeply in debt, and without a railroad, Brownville was abandoned by many residents.

In 1970 the historic importance of Brownville was recognized by its enrollment of the National Register of Historic Places.

Governor Robert W. Furnas
Nebraska State Historical Society

Located: US 136 - city park at center of Brownville.

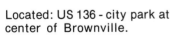

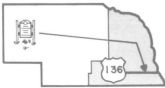

OFFICIAL STATE MAP: M-30
NEMAHA COUNTY

Brick Muir House

Nebraska State Historical Society

Nebraska State Historical Society

R. Valentine Muir

OFFICIAL STATE MAP: M-30
NEMAHA COUNTY

Located: US 136 - a block north of highway in northeastern Brownville.

NEBRASKA HISTORICAL MARKER

MUIR HOUSE

This is the former home of Robert Valentine Muir, an early resident of Brownville. Born in Scotland in 1827, Muir came to America in 1835 and moved to Nebraska in 1856 as Treasurer for the Nebraska Settlement Company. He operated a sawmill, flour business, and ferry. He was also involved in real estate and was a publisher of the **Nebraska Advertiser**.

Muir led an active public life. For years he was a key figure in the Prohibition Party of Nebraska and ran for Governor as its candidate. He died in 1917.

One of Nebraska's most elegant early homes, the house was erected by Muir during 1868-1870. It was built of native Nebraska brick, in the Italianate style. The paneling of butternut, bird's-eye maple, and black walnut consists of native woods cut in Muir's own sawmill, located across the river in Missouri. This important example of our early architecture has been restored by Mrs. Harold D. LeMar.

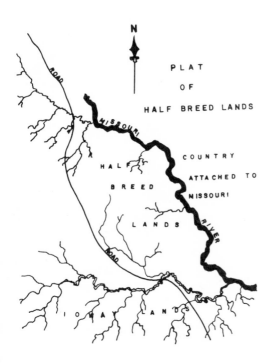

PLAT

OF

HALF BREED LANDS

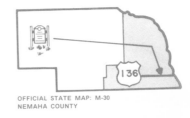

OFFICIAL STATE MAP: M-30
NEMAHA COUNTY

Located: US 136 - ¾ mile east of Auburn.

NEBRASKA
HISTORICAL MARKER

HALF-BREED TRACT

It was an accepted custom for many early fur traders to marry into Indian tribes. As the Indians ceded their lands, the rights of the half-breed descendants were not always identified. This situation was recognized by the government in 1830, by the Prairie Du Chien Treaty which set aside a tract of land for the half-breeds of the Oto, Iowa, Omaha and Santee Sioux tribes.

This tract was located between the Great and Little Nemaha rivers. In 1838, the land was surveyed by John C. McCoy, who placed the western boundary eight miles west of the river instead of ten miles as specified. This caused problems, as later white settlers were to settle on Indian lands west of McCoy's line. Congress ordered the land resurveyed, and in 1858 the McCoy line was made official. On September 10, 1860, Louis Neal received the first patent.

The owners were never required to live on their property and many eventually sold their lands to whites. One of the original survey lines is now partly identified by the Half-Breed Road which runs in a southeast direction from here. The descendants of some pioneer fur traders still live in the area.

NEBRASKA
HISTORICAL MARKER

PERU STATE COLLEGE

Peru State College, originally incorporated as Mount Vernon Seminary, became Nebraska's first state-supported college on June 20, 1867. The school was initially organized and largely financed by local residents, then offered to the Methodist Conference. When the Conference refused, the school was offered to the state.

Called the Nebraska State Normal School, Peru was one of the first of its kind west of the Missouri River. Its first classes as a state school were held on October 24, 1867, with thirty-two students enrolled in the normal department. The campus at that time contained sixty acres of land and one building, Mount Vernon Hall.

The school's purpose as outlined in the Legislative bill was to "instruct young people in the art of teaching and in the various branches that pertain to the good common school education, in mechanic arts, in the arts of husbandry and agricultural chemistry, in the fundamental laws of the United States, and in good citizenship."

During its first one hundred years, Peru State College expanded to a campus of one hundred acres dotted with twenty academic buildings and housing complexes to accommodate an enrollment of more than 1,100 students.

OFFICIAL STATE MAP: M-30
NEMAHA COUNTY

Located: Nebraska 67 - southern campus edge in Peru.

Peru State Normal College, 1909

Nebraska State Historical Society

Nebraska State Historical Society

A few of the survivors of the 1864 Indian Raids included Laura Roper, Danny Marble and Isabella Eubanks.

Located: Nebraska 14 - 9 miles north of Nelson.

OFFICIAL STATE MAP: N-22
NUCKOLLS COUNTY

NEBRASKA
HISTORICAL MARKER

1864 INDIAN RAIDS

During the Civil War many regular troops were withdrawn from Plains military posts to fight in the east. The Sioux, Cheyenne and Arapaho, seizing this opportunity, attempted to drive white settlers from their land.

Beginning on August 7, 1864, the Indians made concerted attacks on stage stations and ranches along the Oregon Trail, hitting nearly every settlement for 400 miles from Julesburg to Big Sandy. Travel ceased for two months.

The most severe attacks were along the upper Little Blue River where about 100 people were killed. Several died at Oak Grove but others escaped and Pawnee Ranch was successfully defended. At "the Narrows" the Eubanks families were attacked and seven killed. Mrs. Eubanks, two children and Miss Laura Roper were taken prisoner and held captive for months. Teamsters were killed, wagon trains burned and ranches were smashed or burned. Settlers fled east to Beatrice and Marysville or northwest to Fort Kearny on the Platte for protection.

Troops and local militia companies attacked and drove back the Indians in the battle of the Little Blue on August 17, 1864. Major raids ceased but skirmishes continued through the fall.

Nebraska State Historical Society
General Stephen W. Kearney

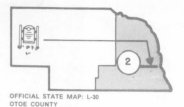

OFFICIAL STATE MAP: L-30
OTOE COUNTY

Located: Nebraska 2 - East Central Avenue and 5th Street in Nebraska City.

NEBRASKA HISTORICAL MARKER

OLD FORT KEARNY

The increase in overland travel after 1843 resulted in the establishment of a chain of military posts across the West to protect the travelers.

Early in 1846 the first of these posts was built by the army in this location near the mouth of Table Creek, an area explored and selected by Colonel Stephen W. Kearny. A two-story blockhouse was erected about ½ block west of here. Subsequently, a number of log huts were built as temporary shelter for the troops.

The Table Creek site was not on the main route of overland traffic and relatively few emigrants passed the fort. The War Department, in 1847, selected a new site on the widely used main branch of the Oregon Trail. Fort Childs, later designated as Fort Kearny, was built near the Platte River, in present day Kearney County.

The Old Fort Kearny area remained important as the beginning of a secondary route of the Oregon Trail, The Nebraska City-Fort Kearny cut off. Nebraska City was started at the site. The blockhouse was used as a printing office, justice court, jail, drugstore and butcher shop. A replica of it was dedicated in 1938.

NEBRASKA CITY

Permanent settlement in this area dates from 1846, with the establishment of old Fort Kearny on Table Creek. Nebraska City, founded in 1854, became an important depot for military and commercial freighting. Pioneer businessmen, such as S. F. Nuckolls, sought to attract freighting interests. In 1858, Alexander Majors, of Russell, Majors and Waddell, decided to use Nebraska City as the point of departure for shipping military supplies west.

Steamboats brought rapidly growing volumes of goods and numbers of people heading west. In 1865, it was reported that up to 40 million pounds of freight were shipped west from Nebraska City.

In 1860, a direct road to new Fort Kearny on the Platte was completed, shortening that journey by forty miles. Known as the Nebraska City-Fort Kearny Cut-off and also as the Great Central Route, the trail was originally marked by a furrow ploughed in the sod. Another name for this trail, the Steam Wagon Road, resulted from an 1862 experiment. That summer, a locomotive-like "Steam Wagon" attempted to haul cargo to Denver, but soon broke down and was abandoned.

With the building of the Union Pacific Railroad, overland freighting from Nebraska City soon gave way to railroad shipment.

Alexander Majors

Nebraska State Historical Society

Located: US 73 - 75 - ½ mile northwest of downtown Nebraska City at rest area.

OFFICIAL STATE MAP: L-30
OTOE COUNTY

Nebraska State Historical Society

The 1862 Steam Wagon was owned by J. R. Brown.

Located: Nebraska 2 - northwestern edge of Syracuse.

OFFICIAL STATE MAP: L-28
OTOE COUNTY

NEBRASKA
HISTORICAL MARKER

NEBRASKA CITY-FORT KEARNY CUTOFF

You are near the old freighting trail of the Nebraska City-Fort Kearny
Cutoff. Prior to railroad construction, thousands of wagons transported
supplies to Fort Kearny and other military posts throughout the West. The
Mormon War and the discovery of gold in the Colorado and Montana
Territories brought Nebraska City to prominence as a freighting center
between 1858-1865. Early freighters used the Ox-Bow Trail which looped
north to the Platte Valley. It provided abundant grass and water but it was
overly long and often plagued by muddy lowlands.

Because of competition from other Missouri River towns, Nebraska City
freighters sought a more direct route. The Nebraska City-Fort Kearny
Cutoff, proposed in 1858 and first traveled in 1860, was first marked by a
plowed furrow. Bridges and improvements were added when the famed
Steam Wagon was brought to Nebraska Territory in 1862. This experiment
failed, but the route continued to be called the "Steam Wagon Road."

Freighting from Nebraska City peaked in 1865 when over 44 million
pounds of supplies were shipped. Construction of the Union Pacific soon
marked the end of major freighting on this road.

Arbor Lodge
State Historical Park

STATE
HISTORICAL
PARK

J. Sterling Morton's home, Arbor Lodge, is located on the west edge of Nebraska City and is one of the most historically significant houses of the West. Morton was acting Governor for a time, then became U.S. Secretary of Agriculture under President Cleveland in 1893. His former home, now a 52-room mansion, and surrounding tracts of ornamental trees and orchard, proclaim Morton's interest in trees. On March 31, 1874, then Governor Robert Furnas issued the first Arbor Day proclamation, giving wide-spread impetus to the holiday and furthering Morton's programs of tree planting. In addition to the mansion, a carriage house contains many examples of early-day horsedrawn vehicles including a stagecoach, surrey, sleigh and other coaches.

Located: Nebraska 2 - western edge of Nebraska City.

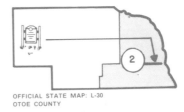

OFFICIAL STATE MAP: L-30
OTOE COUNTY

The historic home of J. Sterling Morton, founder of Arbor Day, is preserved as a memorial at Arbor Lodge State Park near Nebraska City, Nebraska. Here visitors may view over 200 species of trees, shrubs, and garden plants.

Nebraska Game and Parks Commission

STATE
HISTORICAL
PARK

Nebraska State Historical Society

United States Secretary of Agriculture of 1893,
J. Sterling Morton

Secretary Morton's private study has been preserved.

Nebraska Game and Parks Commission

STATE
HISTORICAL
PARK

Nebraska Game and Parks Commission
This is the President's Bedroom of Arbor Lodge. President Cleveland slept here.

Arbor Lodge's dining room was richly decorated.

Nebraska Game and Parks Commission

Besides the gardens and the Arbor Lodge, visitors may view and even ride early-day horse drawn vehicles.

Nebraska Game and Parks Commission

Located: County Courthouse grounds, Holdrege, Nebraska.

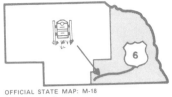

OFFICIAL STATE MAP: M-18
PHELPS COUNTY

NEBRASKA
HISTORICAL MARKER

PHELPS COUNTY

The great immigrant roads to the West which followed the Platte River brought the first settlers to this area. Beginning in the late 1850's, these frontiersmen operated stage stations, road ranches, and trading posts. An August attack upon a wagon train in present northwestern Phelps County, known as the Plum Creek Massacre, was the initial incident of the Indian War of 1864.

Phelps County was organized on April 23, 1873, with the northern town of Williamsburg being named the county seat. The seat of government was moved to Phelps Center in 1879 and again to Holdrege, its present location, in 1883. Early settlers, lured by government homestead lands and cheap railroad lands, were mainly of Swedish descent. Excellence in education, religion, and agriculture was their goal, as it is today.

This area is credited with one of the world's largest underground water supplies. Phelps County is 348,000 acres in size of which 338,300 are farmland. In 1973, the county's centennial year, over 62% of its cropland is watered by 1,041 irrigation wells and over 350 miles of ditches and laterals.

One sample of deep-well irrigation is this Nebraska field of sugar beets under irrigation.
Nebraska State Historical Society

HISTORIC PLATTE VALLEY

Through this valley passed the Oregon Trail, highway for early explorers, fur traders, California-bound gold seekers, freighters, and brave pioneers seeking new homes in the West. Traffic was especially heavy from 1843 to 1866. At times as many as 800 wagons passed this point daily, heading both directions.

The Pony Express passed through the valley, followed by the first telegraph lines. This was also the military road to western destinations. Beginning in 1847, the Mormons broke a new trail on the north side of the Platte.

Indian raids by the Sioux and Cheyenne were severe in the 1860's, and several attacks occurred near here. During the Plum Creek Massacre a few miles west, wagons were burned and several people killed or captured.

Huge herds of buffalo once roamed these prairies, often stopping traffic on the trail. In the 1870's hunters slaughtered them by the thousands.

Today the Platte Valley is one of the nation's rich agricultural areas, disproving the opinion of early explorers who saw the Great Plains only as the Great American Desert.

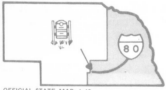

OFFICIAL STATE MAP: L-18
PHELPS COUNTY

Located: I-80 - 2 miles south
of Elm Creek access.

The Overland Pony Express riders often sped past telegraph builders. The telegraph was the cause for the pony express's quick demise.

Nebraska State Historical Society

Located: US 30 - Columbus
Fairgrounds.

OFFICIAL STATE MAP: H-24
PLATTE COUNTY

NEBRASKA
HISTORICAL MARKER

AGRICULTURAL PARK

Due to the generosity of Mrs. Albert Gehner, Mr. Theodore Friedhof, and many other benefactors, this site has become a focal point of agricultural activity in Platte County.

The donation of this land, formerly known as the Browner Farm, and a large sum of money enabled the dreams of several area residents to become reality on June 3, 1941. On that date, a non-profit organization was formed for the purpose of ''encouraging improvement in all things pertaining to agriculture, industry, merchandising, domestic science and good citizenship in Platte County.''

Since that date, county fairs have been held annually under the supervision of a 15-member board of directors, elected from throughout the county. Numerous activities promoting livestock breeding and the work of 4-H and F.F.A. clubs are also held frequently. Thoroughbred horse racing meets are held each summer. Hundreds of college scholarships have been awarded deserving students of the county since the inception of this society, and many donations have been made to worth-while civic projects.

This historical mural may be seen at the Loup River Public Power District, Columbus.

Nebraska State Historical Society

Nebraska State Historical Society

Union Pacific Railroad gangs worked their way across Nebraska in 1867.

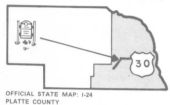

OFFICIAL STATE MAP: I-24
PLATTE COUNTY

Located: US 30 - 1 block
north of elevator at Duncan.

NEBRASKA
HISTORICAL MARKER

1871 DUNCAN 1971

The history of Duncan, Nebraska has been closely associated with overland routes through the Platte and Loup River valleys. The Mormon Trail passed nearby during the mid-19th Century and the first transcontinental railroad was completed to this point in 1866. The early settlers in the area included Swiss and Polish immigrants. In June, 1869, Cherry Hill Post Office was established here. Two years later, in 1871, officials of the Union Pacific Railroad platted the town of Jackson on this site.

In 1879, Jackson was selected as the location for the junction of the Union Pacific and its subsidiary, the Omaha, Niobrara, and Black Hills Railroad. Union Pacific financier, Jay Gould reportedly chose Jackson for the junction because he was angered at the nearby town of Columbus which had promoted construction of a rival railroad into the region. However, an ice jam destroyed the Loup River bridge on the Omaha, Niobrara and Black Hills line in 1881, and the tracks were later relocated to join the Union Pacific at Columbus.

In 1880, Jackson was renamed Duncan and the Village was formally incorporated on March 4, 1913.

Nebraska State Historical Society   Frank North

Nebraska State Historical Society   Luther North

Located: US 81 - south of viaduct, next to Chamber of Commerce in Columbus.

OFFICIAL STATE MAP: H-24
PLATTE COUNTY

NEBRASKA
HISTORICAL MARKER

THE NORTH BROTHERS

The West produced many fighting men and ranking high among them are Frank and Luther North of Columbus, leaders of the legendary Pawnee Scouts. The Pawnee, located at their nearby reservation, were eager to cooperate with the Army in fighting their hereditary enemies the Sioux and Cheyenne. Organized as a fighting unit in 1864, they participated in the Powder River Campaigns of 1865 and 1876-1877 and the Republican River Campaign of 1869. They also guarded the builders of the first transcontinental railroad, 1867-1869. William F. Cody, "Buffalo Bill," later Frank North's ranching partner, first became associated with him in the campaign which culminated with the battle of Summit Springs, 1869.

Frank North was the commander of the Scouts and one of the West's most successful Indian fighters. The Pawnee revered him and knew him as Pani Leshar or Pawnee Chief. He was assisted on most of the campaigns by his brother Luther. The two brothers spoke Pawnee and a mutual respect and affection existed between them and the Indian soldiers. A number of other Columbus men, including Lt. Gustavus G. Becher, served as officers of the Scouts.

The Pawnee moved to Oklahoma in 1875. The North Brothers lived in Columbus the remainder of their lives after having contributed a colorful chapter to the story of the West.

Nebraska State Historical Society

Early in the 1800s George Catlin painted the portrait of Osceola, Black Drink, a Seminole Indian.

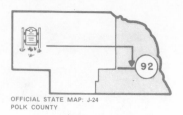

OFFICIAL STATE MAP: J-24
POLK COUNTY

Located: Nebraska 92 eastern edge of Osceola.

NEBRASKA HISTORICAL MARKER

OSCEOLA AND THE EARLY PIONEER
1867-1967

The early settlement of Polk County in 1867 brings us in close touch with the trail of the pioneer. Then from year to year, others came and settlement advanced. These early settlers came by covered wagon, many with ox team. The nearest railroad was 40 miles distant and the roads were trails angling from place to place. The vast expanse of prairie grass, as far as the eye could see was broken only here and there by smoke arising from some sod house on a claim.

Osceola, the county seat and geographical center of Polk County is said to have been named after the Indian Chief Osceola of Florida. It was first located three miles southeast of the present site. The present location was made permanent October 10, 1871. The post office was established June, 1872 and the town was incorporated on August 26, 1881. At this date, Osceola was the terminus of the mail route from Lincoln via Ulysses. The Union Pacific Railroad ran its first train into Osceola June 23, 1879, giving direct communication with the outer world.

Polk County has been the home of three governors, Albinus Nance, John H. Mickey and Ashton C. Shallenberger.

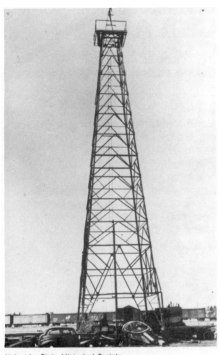

Nebraska State Historical Society

This is a Bucholz Well of the Richardson County oilfields.

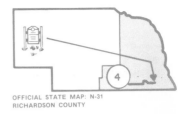

OFFICIAL STATE MAP: N-31
RICHARDSON COUNTY

Located: Nebraska 4 - west of Falls City.

NEBRASKA
HISTORICAL MARKER

FIRST OIL WELL

The first publicized report of oil in Nebraska was an 1883 newspaper account of a "vein of petroleum" discovered in Richardson County. Over the next 57 years, the search for oil consumed thousands of dollars, and hundreds of wells were drilled throughout Nebraska. Traces of oil were reported at various locations across the state, but Nebraska did not have a producing well until 1940.

In 1939 and 1940 the Pawnee Royalty Company had two encouraging but unsuccessful drillings near Falls City. A third well, known as Bucholz No. 1, was begun near here on April 22, 1940. On May 29, 1940, the well began producing and averaged 169-½ barrels daily for the first 60 days.

Bucholz Well No. 1 thus easily qualified for a $15,000 bonus offered by the Nebraska Legislature for the first oil well in the state to produce at least 50 barrels daily for 60 consecutive days. Interestingly, Bucholz No. 1 was located about five miles east of the "vein of petroleum" reported in 1883.

Although today Nebraska's oil production is largely centered in the southwestern panhandle, the pioneer efforts in this area have resulted in a major contribution to the economy of the state.

NEBRASKA
HISTORICAL MARKER

CZECH CAPITAL

Many nationalities blended in America and Nebraska to create our great nation and state. Prominent among them were the Czechs.

They left a land which knew a great history and culture. The first university in Central Europe was established in Prague over 100 years before Columbus discovered America. Throughout generations of wars and oppression the Czech people kept alive their language, music, arts and customs, and they brought them to the New World. Here they live on.

Charles Culek, who came to Nebraska in 1856, was the first permanent Czech settler. The first Czechs came to Saline County in 1865. In all, some 50,000 Czechs settled in Nebraska, most of them from the Province of Bohemia.

They tended to congregate in villages, such as Wilber, officially designated by the Governor as the Czech Capital of Nebraska. Schuyler, Clarkson, Prague, and other towns were mainly settled by Czechs. Like other pioneers, Czechs conquered the hardships of frontier life, and thrived in the new land. Here they found freedom from oppression, and opportunity for their children. These peoples' industry and patriotism, with that of other nationalities, helped to make America and Nebraska great.

Karel Zulek (Charles Culek)
Nebraska State Historical Society

Located: Intersection of Nebraska 41 and 103 - northeast corner of junction at Wilber.

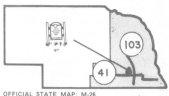

OFFICIAL STATE MAP: M-26
SALINE COUNTY

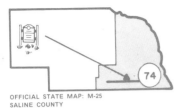

OFFICIAL STATE MAP: M-25
SALINE COUNTY

Located: Nebraska 74 - 1
block east of railroad at
eastern edge of Tobias.

Arizona Historical Society
Ordnance Sergeant Leodegar Schnyder

NEBRASKA HISTORICAL MARKER

SERGEANT LEODEGAR SCHNYDER

Sergeant Leodegar Schnyder, who is buried in nearby Atlanta Center Cemetery, served in the U.S. Army for fifty-three years, longer than any other non-commissioned officer. Thirty-seven years were spent at the same frontier army post.

Born in Switzerland in 1814, Schnyder came to the United States with his parents in 1829. Enlisting in the army in 1837, he saw action in the Seminole War. In 1849 Schnyder's company was ordered to the newly established Fort Laramie, an isolated outpost on the overland trails. During the many years he served there, it was a focal point for emigrant travel and military campaigns, instrumental in the settlement of the West.

In 1852 Schnyder was promoted to Ordnance Sergeant and he later served as garrison postmaster. He was noted for his strict adherance to military regulations. Twice married at the post, he raised his children there. He retired from the army four years after being transferred to New Bedford, Massachusetts in 1886. With his second wife, Julia, he settled on a farm near Tobias, Nebraska, where he died December 19, 1896.

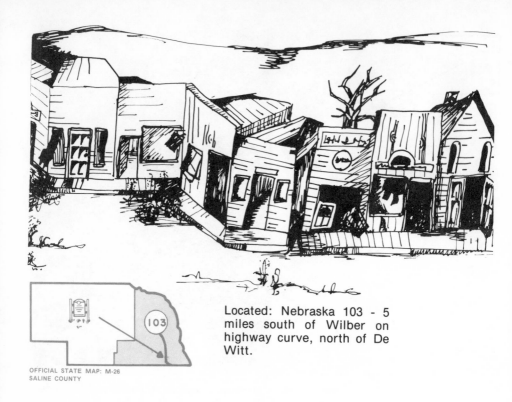

Located: Nebraska 103 - 5 miles south of Wilber on highway curve, north of De Witt.

OFFICIAL STATE MAP: M-26
SALINE COUNTY

NEBRASKA
HISTORICAL MARKER

SWAN CITY

Near here was located the first town and county seat in Saline County. Situated on Swan Creek from which it took its name, Swan City held prominence for only a few years.

The first settlement buildings, including a store and a sawmill, were constructed about 1865. In 1865, William Remington donated the land on which the town was located. The first meeting of the Saline County Commissioners took place there at Cline's Mill on February 17, 1866. Swan City was officially platted on October 8, 1866.

Swan City grew to a community of some 200. Its thriving business section included a hotel. The O'Connor Circus spent a few winters in Swan City.

In 1871, the county seat was moved from Swan City to Pleasant Hill. That same year, the railroad was being built through the Blue River Valley, two and a half miles from Swan City. Most of the town's business community wanted to be near the railroad and moved to either DeWitt or Wilber within two years.

The last vestige of Swan City was the flour mill which continued to operate until it burned in 1891. Swan City thus joined the ranks of ghost towns.

Strategic Aerospace Museum

STATE MUSEUM

From the moment the 82-foot-high Atlas missile comes into view as you approach the Strategic Aerospace Museum until you have absorbed that last bit of nostalgia of a heroic era, your visit to this Nebraska landmark situated on the edge of Offutt Air Force Base near Omaha, will be unforgettable.

Not only will you see an extraordinary collection of U.S. Air Force aircraft that battled in enemy skies to achieve world peace, but also you will be able to share in a lasting monument to the thousands of American flyers who created a proud heritage during a particularly perilous period in our nations's history.

The learning experience gained by taking this unique journey through military aviation history is valuable to young and old alike. One of the B-17 Flying Fortresses that helped destroy the Axis Powers in WWII stands in mute testimony to that violent conflict. A giant, 10-engined, B-36 Peacemaker that provided America's "big stick" during the angry days of the Cold War stretches its 230-foot wingspan across the display area. And a C-54 Skymaster that aided in breaking the back of the Berlin Blockade reposes proudly among her sister airplanes that vaulted the Strategic Air Command into the most awesome air armada the world has ever known.

In addition to touring the aircraft displays, you will want to browse through the Museum's newly-built exhibit hall. Here you will find hundreds of artifacts from a bygone era in American aviation. A pictorial display takes you through more than 60 years of bomber history and you will

OFFICIAL STATE MAP: J-30
SARPY COUNTY

Located: Nebraska 370 about 4 blocks south of highway at southern edge of Bellevue.

Nebraska Department of Economic Development

Aerial view of the Strategic Aerospace Museum Outdoor Displays

enjoy studying many important personal momentos and documents of one of America's most famed military leaders—Gen.Curtis E.LeMay.And you may wish to watch a motion picture on an exciting segment of Air Force history in the exhibit hall's theater.

Hundreds of thousands of visitors have enjoyed the history, memories, and knowledge that the Strategic Aerospace Museum provides. You are cordially invited to share in this experience dedicated to the men of the United States Air Force—past, present and future—and to the men and women of the Strategic Air Command who uphold the Commands' motto, "Peace is our Profession."

Nebraska Department of Economic Development

This is the "Fatman", an atomic bomb similar to the bomb dropped on Nagasaki, Japan, during World War II. The bomb weighed 10,000 pounds.

Nebraska Department of Economic Development

The B-36, ''Peacemaker,'' was SAC's first inter-continental bomber. The 10-engine aircraft was capable of carrying a 50-ton bomb load a distance of 10,000 miles without refueling.

Nebraska Department of Economic Development

The B-47, ''Stratojet,'' was SAC's first big jet bomber seeing duty between 1951 and 1956.

STATE

MUSEUM

General Curtis E. LeMay

U.S. Air Force

Nebraska Game and Parks Commission

This is a B-52. The United States Air Force began using the "Stratofortress" in 1952. Today the aircraft remains as SAC's alert line bomber. Based on its past service the B-52 appears far from obsolete.

STRATEGIC AEROSPACE MUSEUM
... The World's Peace Keeping Force on Display

BOMBERS B-17 Flying Fortress, B-25 Mitchell, B-26 Invader, B-29 Superfortress, B-36 Peacemaker, B-45 Tornado, B-47 Stratojet, B-52 Stratofortress, B-57 Intruder, B-58 Hustler.

FIGHTERS RF-84F Thunderflash, XF-85 Goblin, F-86H Sabrefet, F-101 VOO-doo, F-102 Della Dagger

STRATEGIC SUPPORT C-47 Skytrain, C-54 Skymaster, KC-97 Stratofreighter, C-119 Flying Boxcar, C-124 Globemaster, C-133 Cargomaster, HU-16 Albatross

TRAINERS T-29 Flying Classroom, T-33 Shooting Star

HELICOPTERS HH-19 Chickasaw, CH-21 Workhorse

MISSILES LV-1 Blue Scout, IM-99 BOMARC, AGM-28 Hound Dog, SM-62 Snark, SM-65 Atlas, SM-75 Thor, TITAN

Located: Nebraska 370 - Main Street in front of city hall of Bellevue.

Nebraska State Historical Society **Manuel Lisa**

NEBRASKA HISTORICAL MARKER

BELLEVUE

Bellevue, gateway to the upper Missouri and the fur trade empire, is the oldest continuous settlement in Nebraska. This town was born, became important, almost died, and now in the 20th century, has been revitalized.

Fur traders dealing with the Omaha, Ponca, Oto, and Pawnee, first gave it life. Manuel Lisa probably named it for the beautiful view at the junction of the Platte and Missouri valleys.

In 1823, an Indian Agency was established in Bellevue. Here and at the Peter Sarpy fur trading post travelers such as Prince Maximilian, Carl Bodmer, George Catlin, and John C. Fremont, were welcomed. By 1846 Bellevue was a steamboat landing and the site of an important Indian Mission. Here Francis Burt, the first territorial governor, arrived in 1854, and the first territorial newspaper, the **Nebraska Palladium**, was published.

When the territorial capital was located at Omaha, and the Pacific Railroad was routed to the north, Bellevue faded. In the 1940's the town was rejuvenated when thousands of military personnel, who man the Strategic Air Command center of defense for the western world, made Bellevue their home.

Nebraska State Historical Society · Early engraving of Bellevue

Nebraska State Historical Society

The Reverend William Hamilton family

OFFICIAL STATE MAP: J-30
SARPY COUNTY

Located: Nebraska 370 - Bellevue Boulevard at 20th Avenue, north of Main Street in Bellevue.

NEBRASKA
HISTORICAL MARKER

FIRST PRESBYTERIAN CHURCH

Before the organization of Nebraska Territory in 1854, missions were established among the Indian tribes of this area. In 1850, Rev. Edward McKinney founded the first Presbyterian Church of Nebraska with five members.

He had arrived in Bellevue in 1846 to take over the work of the Indian missions. In 1853, Rev. William Hamilton replaced him as pastor. In 1856, the church body was reorganized and the construction of a permanent edifice was begun. The building was thirty by forty feet and took two years to complete. It was one of the earliest churches built in Nebraska and is the oldest surviving structure built as a church.

Additions to the building were made in 1869, and in 1904 it was enlarged to more than double its original size. The Social Hall was added in 1924. Seating only five hundred, the church became too small for the needs of the congregation. Thus after providing religious services for more than a century, it was replaced in 1958 by a new building.

It has been preserved as a symbol of our pioneer religious heritage.

Presbyterian Mission at Bellevue   Nebraska State Historical Society

NEBRASKA
HISTORICAL MARKER

FONTENELLE BANK - COUNTY COURTHOUSE

This building was constructed in 1856 to serve as the Fontenelle Bank. During the Panic of 1857, the Fontenelle Bank failed as did most of the wildcat banks of the Nebraska Territory.

The legislature of the Territory authorized its purchase in 1860 for public use by Sarpy County and it was acquired by the county in 1861 to become the Sarpy County Courthouse. In 1875 the Sarpy County offices were moved to Papillion.

The building was then used by Bellevue as a Town Hall for more than three quarters of a century, serving the city until 1959, when a municipal building was constructed.

The building is of hand-made Nebraska brick. On the first floor one can still see the vault designed for use by the Fontenelle Bank.

In the history of Nebraska, buildings such as this have given service as the transition has been made from frontier settlements to modern communities. It has been preserved as one of the earliest public buildings in the State of Nebraska.

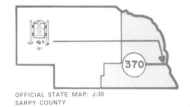

OFFICIAL STATE MAP: J-30
SARPY COUNTY

Located: Nebraska 370 - Main and Mission Streets at Bellevue.

Nebraska State Historical Society

Fontenelle Bank, Bellevue

THE GREAT PLATTE VALLEY

Here is the great Platte Valley, Highway to the West. On these nearby bluffs prehistoric Indians built their homes. The Pawnee and Oto established large earthlodge villages near here.

As you travel west in the valley you will follow the route of the Indians, white explorers, and the early trails to the western United States. In 1820, an exploring party under Major Stephen Long followed the Platte Valley to the Rocky Mountains, as did an 1826 expedition under General William Ashley. By 1830, the valley had become the major supply route for fur traders in the Rocky Mountains.

Beginning in 1847, the Mormons on their way to Utah followed a trail along the north side of the Platte. The Oregon Trail reached the Platte 150 miles west of here and followed the south side of the river. By the late 1850's, it was estimated that 90% of all traffic which crossed the Plains followed the Platte.

The famous Pony Express followed the Platte Valley, as did the first transcontinental telegraph line. By 1869, the first transcontinental railroad was completed and it, too, followed the valley, opening the land along the river for permanent settlement.

Major Stephen H. Long

Nebraska State Historical Society

Located: I-80 west - rest area southwest of Gretna.

OFFICIAL STATE MAP: J-28
SARPY COUNTY

OFFICIAL STATE MAP: J-30
SARPY COUNTY

Located: US 73 - 75 - 1 mile
north of the Platte River at
La Platte access south of
Bellevue.

Nebraska State Historical Society

Chief Itan

NEBRASKA
HISTORICAL MARKER

OTO MISSION

The mission established by Moses Merrill about three miles west of here was an early attempt to make Christianity a part of daily lives of the Oto and Missouri Indians.

Merrill reached Bellevue in 1833 and visited the Oto village in present Saunders County. In September, 1835 the Merrill family, in the service of the Baptist Missionary Union, were located in a log cabin and school house the government provided on the Platte. Led by Chief Itan, part of the Oto and Missouri built a village near the Mission. As the Mission developed, Merrill prepared a spelling book, a reader, and hymnals in the Oto language. More buildings were erected and a blacksmith and farmer were added to the staff.

The Oto were plagued by diminishing game supplies and demoralized by liquor. On April 28, 1837, Itan was killed in an Indian feud, and his successor was unable to maintain the village at the Mission.

Merrill died on February 6, 1840, and was buried at St. Mary, on the east bank of the Missouri opposite Bellevue. Today a stone fireplace and chimney remain at the mission site.

Nebraska State Historical Society

Remains of
Oto Mission

SAUNDERS COUNTY

Saunders County was originally Oto Indian territory, and a large earthlodge village under Chief Itan was located here during the early historic period. Later, the Pawnee established villages in the area and in 1855 held peace conferences with General John M. Thayer.

The Ox-Bow Trail, the primary route from Nebraska City to Fort Kearny in 1846-1859, passed through this area. Pioneers first settled here in 1856 and 1857. The county's organization was approved in 1867 and the county seat located at Ashland. Wahoo was surveyed three years later and became the county seat in 1873. The origin of the name "Wahoo" is uncertain, but it is probably derived from an Oto word.

In 1883 Swedish settlers in Wahoo established a school which eventually became Luther Junior College. When Luther merged with Midland College in Fremont, the Wahoo campus was sold. In 1965 it became the site of John F. Kennedy College.

Among Wahoo's prominent native sons are artist Clarence W. Anderson, geneticist and Nobel Prize winner George Beadle, baseball player "Wahoo Sam" Crawford, composer Howard Hanson and motion picture producer Darryl F. Zanuck.

Howard H. Hanson, Composer of "Song of Democracy"

Nebraska State Historical Society

Located: US 77 - Courthouse green in Wahoo.

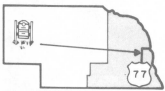

OFFICIAL STATE MAP: I-27
SAUNDERS COUNTY

NEBRASKA
HISTORICAL MARKER

STANTON COUNTY

Named for Secretary of War Edwin M. Stanton in 1863, Jacob Hoffman and Francis Scott filed the first homestead applications in the county on November 18, 1865. The first farms, however, were those of Charles and Mitchell Sharp, who homesteaded near here in the autumn of 1865. This fertile region, enhanced by the Elkhorn River, attracted settlers of German, Norwegian, Czech, Irish Canadian and Swedish origin.

The town of Stanton, platted in 1870, was incorporated in 1881. The Fremont, Elkhorn and Missouri Valley Railroad was built through the county in 1879. The following year the village of Pilger was platted. Named for Peter Pilger, who owned the original townsite, it was incorporated in 1887.

The first large scale farming in the county was the "Township Farm" of Walter Cragg and Ephraim Clark. The farm was divided into four sections, one for crops, one for orchards, and the remaining two used for the raising of swine and cattle. The "Township Farm" attested to the versatility of the region, which makes Stanton County a most productive agricultural area today.

Secretary of War Edwin M. Stanton
Nebraska State Historical Society

Located: US 275 - 3 miles west of Pilger.

OFFICIAL STATE MAP: F-25
STANTON COUNTY

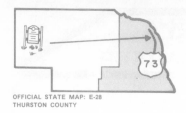

OFFICIAL STATE MAP: E-28
THURSTON COUNTY

Located: US 73 - near Community Building at Macy.

Nebraska State Historical Society

Joseph LaFlesche, "Iron Eyes"

NEBRASKA
HISTORICAL MARKER

OMAHA TRIBE

This was the homeland of the Omaha Tribe long before white settlers came to the Great Plains. By 1750, the Omaha occupied a large region in northeastern Nebraska and northwestern Iowa. The name "Omaha" means "those going against the wind or current" and may refer to a traditional migration up the Missouri River by the ancestors of the present tribe. Lewis and Clark, in 1804, recorded that the Omaha lived here and noted the grave of Chief Blackbird. By a treaty in 1854, the Omaha gave up much of their territory, except for the area of the present reservation.

The Omaha were a peaceful people who lived by agriculture and hunting. During the trying years in the nineteenth century, they were guided by such forward-looking and influential leaders as Big Elk and Joseph La Flesche (Iron Eye). The tribe never took up arms against the flood of white settlers. A number of Omaha served in Nebraska military units as early as the Civil War.

Today, the Omaha people continue to live on their traditional homelands where their ancestors farmed, hunted, and are buried.

Located: US 73 - 1 mile south
of Winnebago and just south
of Winnebago Agency.

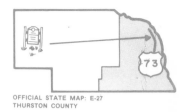

NEBRASKA
HISTORICAL MARKER

WINNEBAGO SCOUTS

In 1863, the Winnebago Indians were moved from their home in
Minnesota to a barren reservation in Dakota Territory. Groups of
Winnebago soon moved down the Missouri River to the Omaha
Reservation in Nebraska. In March, 1865, the Winnebago used their own
funds to purchase land from the Omaha. That land is now the Winnebago
Reservation.

In early 1865, about 75 members of the Winnebago Tribe enlisted in the
Nebraska Volunteers. Known as Company "A", Omaha Scouts, the unit
took an active part in quelling the Indian uprising of 1865 and 1866. This
army service exemplified the Winnebago's desire for peace and good
relationships between the Indians and the white settlers.

In the summer of 1866, upon the return of the Winnebago veterans, a
homecoming festival was held. Shortly thereafter, Chief Little Priest died
of wounds received in army service. An annual memorial celebration is
held in remembrance of his sacrifice. The year following his death, Little
Priest's service flag was raised as a symbol of the tribe's allegiance to their
country. This ceremony remains an important part of each celebration.
Later the gatherings became known as the Annual Pow-wow.

To the honor of these brave and noble forebearers with their rare wisdom
and foresight, do we, the remnants of once a proud nation, dedicate this
marker.

This group of Winnebago Chiefs includes: (front row left) Young Prophet,
Whirling Thunder, White Breast, Little Decorah and Little Hill. Standing
behind the chiefs are Major F. G. Dewitt, Robert Furnas, Alex Payer and
Mirchell (sic) St. Cyn.

Nebraska State Historical Society

NEBRASKA
HISTORICAL MARKER

DESOTO TOWNSITE

The town of DeSoto was platted on this site in 1854 and incorporated in 1855. Steamboating on the Missouri was then in its heyday. DeSoto provided a landing for passengers and goods. A number of boats sank nearby, notably the **Cora** and **Bertrand**. Ambitious citizens advanced plans to make DeSoto a ''gateway to the West'' - first by operating a ferry in 1857 and later by promoting a railroad to connect DeSoto with Fremont. A track was laid as far as present Blair. By 1857 DeSoto had grown to several hundred. Fifteen businesses flourished, including hotels, saloons, stores, newspapers, banks. The town was county seat from 1858 to 1866.

Its decline began in 1859 with a great exodus of residents to the Colorado gold fields. Following the Panic of 1857 its three banks closed. The Sioux City and Pacific Railroad, after buying the DeSoto line's franchise, chose to cross the river three miles north of DeSoto and in 1869 established Blair. DeSoto's hopes for growth were blasted. Its citizens left for other communities, a number to become figures of prominence in judicial, political, and financial circles in Nebraska. Today the Fort Calhoun Power Station is in the area where once flowed the Missouri River.

Located: US 73 - 5 miles north of Ft. Calhoun.

OFFICIAL STATE MAP: H-29
WASHINGTON COUNTY

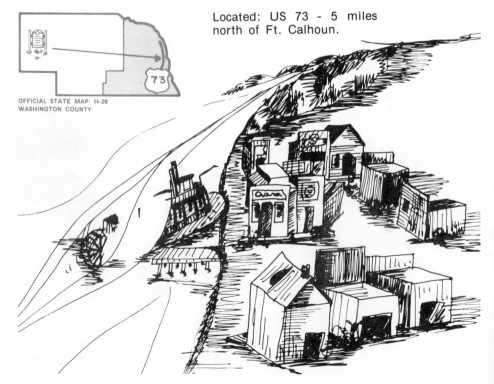

NEBRASKA
HISTORICAL MARKER

STEAMBOAT BERTRAND

During the mid-nineteenth century, steamboats played a major role in the settlement and development of the nation. In March 1865 the fully laden steamwheeler **Bertrand** left St. Louis under the command of Captain James Yore. The cargo of general merchandise and mercury, used in the refinement of gold, was bound for the frontier mining towns near Fort Benton, Montana Territory, at the headwaters of the Missouri.

On April 1, 1865 the 161-foot vessel struck a snag less than a mile from the village of DeSoto, Nebraska Territory. The site of the wreck is now part of the DeSoto National Wildlife Refuge. Although the boat sank in ten minutes, no lives were lost. The **Bertrand** was one of more than 400 steamboats wrecked on the Missouri during the riverboat era.

In 1967 salvors in cooperation with the federal government began a successful search for the **Bertrand**. The excavation was completed in October 1969 after 150 tons of cargo had been removed. The varied and precisely dated contents provide important research and interpretative resources after 103 years. On March 24, 1969 the historic importance of the **Bertrand** was recognized with its entry into the National Register of Historic Places.

The excavating of the Steamer Bertrand began to reveal historic finds in the Spring of 1970. Nebraska State Historical Society

Located: US 30 - 3 miles east of Missouri River Bridge at Blair, in Iowa. Marker is 3½ miles southwest in DeSoto National Wildlife Refuge.

OFFICIAL STATE MAP: H-29
WASHINGTON COUNTY

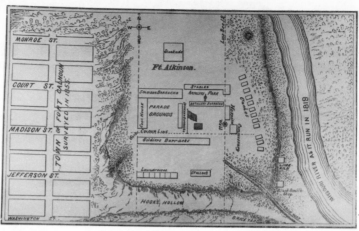

Nebraska State Historical Society

Fort Atkinson, established in 1819, was the first fort built in Nebraska.

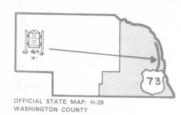

OFFICIAL STATE MAP: H-29
WASHINGTON COUNTY

Located: US 13 - northern side of Washington County Historical Society's Museum in Fort Calhoun.

NEBRASKA
HISTORICAL MARKER

FORT ATKINSON

Civilization came to the west bank of the Missouri with establishment of Fort Atkinson in 1820 about a half mile southeast of here. Named after its founder, General Henry Atkinson, this western-most Fort protected the frontier's developing commerce.

Established as a temporary camp in 1819, Fort Atkinson was the largest and strongest outpost above St. Louis. The permanent post went up a year later on the site of Lewis and Clark's Council with the Oto and Missouri Indians.

From Fort Atkinson troops under the command of Col. Henry Leavenworth moved up the Missouri River in 1823 to punish the Arikara Indians after an attack on William H. Ashley's fur trading party. Members of the garrison ascended the river in 1825 on a mission of peace, participating in a series of treaties with the Indians.

This spearhead of white civilization was abandoned in 1827. But in seven years Fort Atkinson had brought the first school, the first white family life, a library, a sawmill, a brickyard, a grist mill, and large-scale agriculture to the west bank of the Missouri.

Nebraska State Historical Society
General Henry Atkinson

STATE
HISTORICAL
PARK

OFFICIAL STATE MAP: H-29
WASHINGTON COUNTY

Located: US 73 - 2 blocks south of post office in Fort Calhoun.

NEBRASKA
HISTORICAL MARKER

FORT ATKINSON

From 1820 to 1827, the nation's largest and most westerly military post occupied this site, the earlier scene of Lewis and Clark's Council Bluff. In late 1819, troops under Colonel Henry Atkinson established Cantonment Missouri along the river near here. In 1820, a permanent post was built here on the bluffs and named Fort Atkinson. The post's population of over 1000 included military personnel of the elite Rifle Regiment and Sixth Infantry, some of their families, and other civilians. The Sixth U.S. Infantry occupied Fort Atkinson when it was abandoned in 1827.

The fortification consisted of a rectangular arrangement of one-story barracks fashioned of horizontal logs. The structures faced inward upon an enclosed parade ground with loopholes on the exterior walls. Four entrances were located near the center of the four walls. Cannons were mounted in the bastions at the northwest and southeast corners. A massively-built powder magazine occupied the center of the enclosed area.

Outside the fortification were located a large council house for negotiating with the Indians, a gristmill, a schoolhouse, sawmill and other buildings. A brick kiln produced thousands of bricks. Fort Atkinson represents an important early step in opening the West.

Fort Atkinson
State Historical Park

In 1819, the Yellowstone Expedition was sent out to establish a chain of outposts from the mouth of the Missouri River to the Yellowstone River. Its basic purpose was to protect U.S. fur trade and exert American influence over the vast area acquired in the Louisiana Purchase of 1803.

Fort Atkinson was established as a military post as a result of the Yellowstone Expedition of 1819.

The Yellowstone party established Cantonment Missouri about 1½ miles north of the site of Fort Atkinson and spent the winter of 1819-20 there. Sickness and bitter cold claimed the lives of over 100 members of the expedition, and a disastrous spring flood prompted a move from the bottom lands first selected for the encampment to the present site on the valley terrace above the flood plain.

In the meantime, Congress abandoned the idea of a chain of forts for economy reasons, and expedition goals were reduced to the construction of a single permanent fort on the Missouri River. Thus, Fort Atkinson was the only permanent outpost built by the Yellowstone Expedition.

It was the largest post in the west, with a garrison of over 1,000 soldiers during its active period. Such a large garrison exerted a positive influence on the Indians and European traders. Among units stationed there were the elite Rifle Regiment and the famed "Fighting Sixth" Infantry. The two units were later consolidated into one regiment.

Largely self-sufficient, soldiers and civilians at the post produced bricks, lime, sawed lumber, and cultivated several hundred acres of land, proving the area capable of supporting extensive farming and livestock operations.

The fort was abandoned in 1827, and the troops were transferred to Jefferson Barracks near St. Louis, Missouri.

Fortunately, several diaries, letters, and extensive official records provide research material on Atkinson, including a detailed plan of the stockade drawn by the post engineer in 1820. Extensive archaeological excavations during the 1970's of such features as bastions, gates, and buildings will aid in accurate reconstruction of the fort. The only known picture of the fort was painted by Karl Bodmer in 1832 after the post was already in ruins.

All the materials are important, since most physical evidence of the fort was destroyed by fire or removed. The Mormons used bricks from the fort ruins for their quarters north of the site in the mid 1800's. Other settlers entering the region also used the brick and stone for building purposes during the 1850's and 1860's.

The area was acquired by the Nebraska Game and Parks Commission in cooperation with the Fort Atkinson Foundation in 1963. It is undergoing continuing development and interpretation. Visitors are welcome to explore the site, tour the museum, and hike along the bluffs that overlook the channel where the mighty Missouri River flowed 150 years ago.

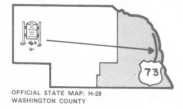

OFFICIAL STATE MAP: H-29
WASHINGTON COUNTY

Located: US 73 - east of Fort Calhoun.

STATE
HISTORICAL
PARK

Nebraska State Historical Society

In 1919, local residents of Fort Calhoun re-enacted the 1819 founding of Fort Atkinson. Above several men are costumed to portray Indian fur traders. Below, fur traders, military officers and Indians add their touch to the centennial celebration.

Nebraska State Historical Society

STATE
HISTORICAL
PARK

Nebraska State Historical Society

In 1956 a basement to one of the Fort Atkinson buildings was excavated.

This is a 1962 painting of Fort Atkinson by Herbert Thomas.

Nebraska State Historical Society

NEBRASKA
HISTORICAL MARKER

WAYNE

Wayne, the county seat of Wayne County, was laid out by the St. Paul and Sioux City Railroad in June 1881. City and county were named for "Mad" Anthony Wayne, a Revolutionary War general. The first settlers arrived in the eastern part of the county in 1868. Some were homesteaders; the first claim was that of Colonel B. F. Whitten near Wakefield in that year. Much of the unbroken prairie land was bought by land speculators, some of it for as little as fifty cents per acre, and sold again to settlers.

When the county was organized in 1870, LaPorte, about six miles southeast of Wayne, was named the county seat. The railroad was extended through the county in 1881-1882 but missed LaPorte and passed through Wayne. The settlers voted to move the county seat and LaPorte became a ghost town.

Wayne has had a college since 1887, when the Lutheran Academy was established. Classes were conducted there until 1890. Nebraska Normal College was founded in 1891 with Professor James M. Pile of Fremont as president. John G. Neihardt, Poet Laureate of Nebraska, was one of the early students. In 1909 the school was purchased by the state and continued as a teachers college. Since 1963 it has been called Wayne State College.

Professor James Madison Pile
Nebraska State Historical Society

Located: Nebraska 35 - 1 mile east of Wayne at airport.

OFFICIAL STATE MAP: E-26
WAYNE COUNTY

Aerial view of Wayne State Teachers College

Nebraska State Historical Society

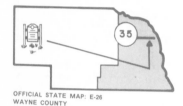

OFFICIAL STATE MAP: E-26
WAYNE COUNTY

Located: Nebraska 35 - on campus green in Wayne.

NEBRASKA HISTORICAL MARKER

WAYNE STATE COLLEGE

The Nebraska Normal College was founded on this site in 1891 as a private institution. It was largely the creation of one man, Professor James M. Pile. The State Legislature in 1909 appropriated funds to purchase the campus, and in 1910 the College opened under State auspices. Its original mission was the same as that of its predecessor college--teacher education in a two-year curriculum. Wayne State College became a four-year degree granting institution in 1921. It has since expanded its program to include study leading to liberal arts and Master's degrees.

The cornerstone nearby came from the Commerce and Arts Building, which was located in the vicinity of this marker. The bell came from the first building of the Nebraska Normal College. John G. Neihardt, later Poet Laureate of Nebraska, rang this bell in the 1890's to signal times for dismissal and convening of classes. With this employment he earned most of his college expense money. In its present location the bell was rung for many years to announce victories in inter-collegiate athletics.

Wayne State College is proud of its graduates, among them outstanding educators, members of the United States Congress, and a governor of Nebraska.

Located: US 136 - Court-
house green in Red Cloud.

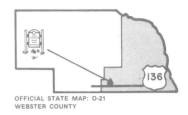

OFFICIAL STATE MAP: O-21
WEBSTER COUNTY

NEBRASKA
HISTORICAL MARKER

1871 WEBSTER COUNTY 1971

On April 10, 1871, Acting Governor William James issued a proclamation calling for the organization of Webster County, with officials to be elected nine days later. The dugout of Silas Garber, later to serve as Nebraska's governor, was the polling place and forty-five votes were cast. A portion of Garber's claim, future Red Cloud, was voted the county seat.

When the first settlers of the county had arrived the previous year, the Republican Valley was the center of the West's great buffalo ranges, still traversed by Indians while on their tribal hunts. Within a very few years, however, those times were gone, and, with the arrival of the railroad in 1879, Webster County was rapidly settled by thousands of homesteaders, ending the frontier era.

Webster County is part of a prosperous mixed-farming region, with numerous irrigated farms, while the rolling divide country has provided rich lands for grazing. The faith of the pioneers, that Webster County would prove to be a wealthy, agricultural home, is proven by the surrounding countryside.

Captain Silas Garber
was the first probate
judge and twice a
governor of Nebraska.
Nebraska State Historical Society

Garber Dug-out House, Webster County
Nebraska State Historical Society

117

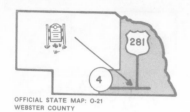

OFFICIAL STATE MAP: O-21
WEBSTER COUNTY

Located: Intersection of US 281 and Nebraska 4 - 15 miles north of Red Cloud.

Nebraska State Historical Society

Willa Sibert Cather, 1893

NEBRASKA HISTORICAL MARKER

CATHERLAND

Here on the Divide between the Republican and the Little Blue lived some of the most courageous people of the frontier. Their fortunes and their loves live again in the writings of Willa Cather, daughter of the plains and interpreter of man's growth in these fields and in the valleys beyond.

On this beautiful, ever-changing land, man fought to establish a home. In her vision of the plow against the sun, symbol of the beauty and importance of work, Willa Cather caught the eternal blending of earth and sky.

Willa Cather wrote from her heart the wonderful tales she heard and the vital drama she saw in her growing years. In her books those she knew and admired live forever. **My Antonia**, earth mother of the plains, grew to maturity, loved, worked, and died within a few miles of this spot, yet she is known and cherished all over the world.

''The history of every country begins in the heart of a man or a woman.'' The history of this land began in the heart of Willa Cather.

NEBRASKA
HISTORICAL MARKER

1871 RED CLOUD 1971

Red Cloud, named for the Oglala Sioux chief, was founded early in 1871 on homestead land filed upon by Silas Garber and company July 17, 1870, at Beatrice, the nearest land office. It is one of the oldest communities in the Republican Valley. When Webster County was organized, Red Cloud was voted the county seat at the first county election, April 19, 1871. The election was held in the dugout of Silas Garber, Nebraska's governor, 1875-1879.

The mainline of the Burlington and Missouri River Railway reached here in 1879, accelerating immigration from the East and abroad, bringing together a colorful variety of cultural heritages. During the 1880's Red Cloud served as a division center for the railroad. The architectural design of Webster Street was established during that prosperous time when many of the first frame and log structures were replaced by more elaborate buildings of brick and stone.

Red Cloud was the childhood home of Willa Cather and it is known throughout the world as the setting for her six Nebraska novels and numerous short stories. The pioneers she knew in the town and on the nearby farms live on in her writings.

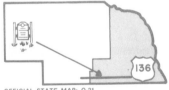

OFFICIAL STATE MAP: O-21
WEBSTER COUNTY

Located: US 136 - city park in Red Cloud.

This is the town of Willa Cather's childhood - Red Cloud.

Nebraska State Historical Society

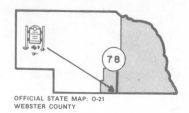

Located: Nebraska 78 - Main Street in Guide Rock.

Nebraska State Historical Society

Major Zebulon Montgomery Pike

NEBRASKA HISTORICAL MARKER

REPUBLICAN PAWNEE VILLAGE

Near here was a large permanent village of the Republican band of the Pawnee tribe which may have been occupied as early as 1777. On September 25, 1806, Lieutenant Zebulon M. Pike visited the village with a small party of soldiers. He was greeted by Chief Characterish and 300 horsemen. The American party found that the village had been recently visited by a large Spanish expedition from Santa Fe.

Pike set up camp with rifle pits on the north bank of the river opposite the village. He persuaded the Pawnee to lower a Spanish flag and raise the American flag. After holding peace conferences between the Osage, Kansa and Pawnee, Pike served notice the land was now a part of the United States and the Spanish would be forbidden in the area. On October 7th, the American party defied the warnings of the Pawnee not to travel toward the Spanish settlements. He and his party were captured by the Spanish but were eventually released.

A short distance downstream from the village site is one of the five "sacred places" of the Pawnee. It is known as **Pa-hur'** to the Pawnee or "hill that points the way" and as Guide Rock to the whites.

NEBRASKA
HISTORICAL MARKER

THE SANDHILLS

and

CENTRAL NEBRASKA

STATE
HISTORICAL
PARK

OFFICIAL STATE MAP: M-10
CHASE COUNTY

Located: US 6 - to Imperial.
State Spur 15A - 4 miles
southwest of Imperial.

Nebraska Game and Parks Commission

Today Champion Mill is the only water-powered mill still operable in Nebraska.

NEBRASKA
HISTORICAL MARKER

CHAMPION WATER-POWERED MILL

Champion, on the Frenchman River, is the site of probably the oldest functioning water-powered mill in Nebraska. Preliminary construction on the mill was begun in the fall of 1886. The work was completed and the mill placed in operation by late 1888. The original mill burned in the early 1890's, but was soon rebuilt. It has remained in use since that time.

The construction of flour mills reflected Chase County's transition from ranching to farming. Dominated by ranching in its early years, the county saw a heavy influx of farmers after 1885. The construction of mills symbolized the new dominance of farming.

Chase County was formally organized in 1886. Imperial remained the county seat through three elections, although Champion sought support because of its advantageous location on the Frenchman River.

Chase County was named for Champion S. Chase, Nebraska's first Attorney-General. Originally known as Hamilton, the town of Champion was renamed in honor of the same Champion S. Chase in 1887.

Imperial Republican

On September 26, 1969, Imperial residents gathered for the deed transaction ceremony that made the Mill a state historical facility.

Mr. and Mrs. Carl Hill, left, presented deed for Champion Mill to Jack O'Keefe, head of State Game and Parks Commission realty division. He, in turn, gave them a check for $7,500.

Imperial Republican

STATE
HISTORICAL
PARK

Nebraska Game and Parks Commission

In its "hey day" Champion Mill ground feed, flour and breakfast cereals.

STATE
HISTORICAL
PARK

After 77 years of continuous service, Champion Mill is under development as a state historical park. The history of grain production and milling closely follows Nebraska's earliest development factors. Champion Mill, located in southwestern Nebraska, does not grind grain anymore, but its wheels still turn for visitors.

Nebraska Game and Parks Commission

OFFICIAL STATE MAP: B-14
CHERRY COUNTY

Located: US 20 - 1 mile
southeast of Valentine.

Nebraska State Historical Society
John J. Pershing

NEBRASKA
HISTORICAL MARKER

FORT NIOBRARA

When a Sioux Indian reservation was established north of here in Dakota Territory in 1878, early settlers in the region grew fearful of attack. They requested military protection, and in 1880 Fort Niobrara was built a few miles east of present-day Valentine. There was no later Indian trouble in the immediate area, and the Ghost Dance religion in the early 1880's brought the last major Indian scare. Among the officers once stationed at Fort Niobrara were John J. Pershing, later commander of U.S. forces in World War I, and Frederick W. Benteen, a survivor of General Custer's ill-fated staff.

Fort Niobrara was an active post until 1906. In 1912 part of the original military reservation was set aside as a national game preserve. It has since become Fort Niobrara National Wildlife Refuge, with ranges maintaining sizable herds of buffalo, elk and Texas longhorn cattle.

Cherry County, a center of cattle production, was organized in 1883 and named for Lieutenant Samuel A. Cherry, a Fort Niobrara officer killed in the line of duty. Valentine, founded in 1882, was named for early-day congressman E. K. Valentine.

Fort Niobrara

Nebraska State Historical Society

BROKEN BOW

A discarded Indian bow suggested the name for a town. Wilson Hewitt, an early homesteader, had applied for the location of a post office on his place. Approving the location, the government rejected Hewitt's first three suggested names as being too similar to names previously approved. Remembering a broken bow recently found nearby, Hewitt then submitted the name "Broken Bow," which the Post Office Department readily approved.

This area was the center of what eventually came to be known as the Sod House Frontier. As homesteaders began to enter this largely treeless region, they made their first homes of prairie sod, which they cut into strips. Early churches, schools and some business places were also made of sod. Homesteaders used sod to construct corrals, henhouses, corn cribs, wind breaks, and even pig pens. One enterprising Custer County resident even constructed a full two storied sod house while others were usually single story or story and a half.

As the region became more settled, Broken Bow grew, and, in 1882, became the county seat of Custer County. That same year, Mr. Jess Gandy donated the sites for the county court house and for the city square.

Nebraska State Historical Society

Wilson Hewitt

Located: Nebraska 2 - Courthouse green at Broken Bow.

OFFICIAL STATE MAP: I-17
CUSTER COUNTY

Located: Nebraska 40
Morgan Park in Callaway.

Milo Young, Rancher   Nebraska State Historical Society

NEBRASKA
HISTORICAL MARKER

CUSTER COUNTY'S FIRST COURTHOUSE

Custer County, named in memory of General George Armstrong Custer, was organized July 27, 1877. Frontiersmen and pioneer ranchers had been living in the area since 1872. Earlier, soldiers from Fort McPherson and settlers from the Platte River counties had regularly made hunting expeditions here, for its river valleys were noted feeding grounds for deer, elk and antelope.

The log ranch house of Milo F. Young, then located in Section 23, Township 15N, Range 22W, was designated as the temporary county seat. Built in 1876, it officially served as the county courthouse for seven years, though most of the county records were kept in the homes of the officials. In it, on December 17, 1880, were held the hearings which lead to the Olive-Fisher trial for the lynching of Mitchell and Ketchum, one of history's most noted feuds between ranchers and homesteaders.

The log house continued to serve as a private residence for many years but was finally abandoned. At the request of several community organizations in 1933, the Young estate donated the house to the village of Callaway, and it was moved here to Morgan Park.

THE NEBRASKA STATE GRANGE

The National Grange of the Patrons of Husbandry was organized in Washington, D.C. in 1867. During the 1870's, it was the major voice of the American farmer and its social, educational, and fraternal activities brightened farm life. "Granger Laws", enacted by state governments, established the pattern for modern America's regulated free enterprise economy.

The Nebraska State Grange was organized in 1872, but errors in its co-operative ventures and the rise of the Farmers Alliance led to its decline. The Grange movement was re-established with the organization of Custer Center Grange near here in February, 1911. The State Grange was reorganized in Broken Bow, November, 1911. Local Granges have spread over the state and are noted for contributions to community life and sound farm policy. Custer Center Grange continues as the oldest Grange organization in Nebraska.

James D. Ream--first Master of both the Custer Center and Nebraska State Granges--was one of Nebraska's leading agricultural pioneers. One of the first settlers in this valley in 1880, he developed his homestead into the beautiful Cedar Lawn Farm.

James D. Ream, First Master of Nebraska State Grange

Nebraska State Historical Society

Located: Nebraska 2 - 6 miles northwest of Broken Bow.

OFFICIAL STATE MAP: I-17
CUSTER COUNTY

NEBRASKA
HISTORICAL MARKER

CENTRAL PLATTE VALLEY

Here in Dawson County, much of the early history is concerned with the pioneer trails to the west. The Mormon Trail to Utah and the first transcontinental railroad passed through here on the north side of the Platte River; the Oregon Trail and the Pony Express followed the south side of the Platte.

Indian trouble was not uncommon here in the early days of settlement. The Plum Creek Massacre occurred in 1864 when Sioux Indians attacked a wagon train, killing several men and taking prisoners at a site near here in Phelps County. Also near here, in 1867 a group of Cheyenne led by Chief Turkey Leg cut the telegraph line, derailed a locomotive, and killed several Union Pacific Railroad employees. The Army's Pawnee Indian Scouts, commanded by Major Frank North, came to the rescue and drove away the hostile Cheyenne.

Permanent settlements began to appear after the construction of the railroad. One of the earliest of these was Plum Creek, later renamed Lexington. The first settlers moved there from a stage station on the south side of the river shortly before the coming of the railroad.

OFFICIAL STATE MAP: K-16
DAWSON COUNTY

Located: I-80 East - Dawson County Rest Area.

Major Frank North
Nebraska State Historical Society

Nebraska State Historical Society

Plum Creek, Dawson County

OFFICIAL STATE MAP: K-16
DAWSON COUNTY

Located: I-80 West - Dawson
County Rest Area.

NEBRASKA HISTORICAL MARKER

CENTRAL PLATTE VALLEY

Here in Dawson County, much of the early history is concerned with the pioneer trails to the west. The Mormon Trail to Utah and the first transcontinental railroad passed through here on the north side of the Platte River; the Oregon Trail and the Pony Express followed the south side of the Platte.

Indian trouble was not uncommon here in the early days of settlement. The Plum Creek Massacre occurred in 1864 when Sioux Indians attacked a wagon train, killing several men and taking prisoners at a site near here in Phelps County. Also near here, in 1867 a group of Cheyenne led by Chief Turkey Leg cut the telegraph line, derailed a locomotive, and killed several Union Pacific Railroad employees.

The town of Cozad, northwest of here, lies directly on the 100th Meridian, considered an important goal in the building of the first transcontinental railroad. When the tracks reached this point in 1866, some 250 businessmen, senators, congressmen and other notables came here to celebrate. The 100th Meridian is often cited as the ''line of aridity,'' west of which rainfall is usually insufficient to support nonirrigated agriculture.

NEBRASKA
HISTORICAL MARKER

THE 100TH MERIDIAN

The 100th Meridian is the 100th longitudinal line west of Greenwich, England which was set by Congress as a major goal in building the first transcontinental railroad. Construction of the Union Pacific reached the Meridian on October 5, 1866. The first passenger train brought 250 notables, including railroad and territorial officials, congressmen and newspapermen to celebrate the event here on October 26, 1866. A large wooden sign designating "The 100th Meridian, 247 miles west of Omaha," which stood close to the track for many years, was replaced in 1933 by the Cozad Chapter of D. A. R.

In 1879 Major John Wesley Powell in his report for the United States Geological Survey recognized the 100th Meridian as the natural demarcation line between the humid east and the arid west. Evaporation from the gulf waters supplies most of the rainfall for the eastern half of the United States. West of this line precipitation, which comes largely from the Pacific, is insufficient for agricultural needs without irrigation. Here on the 100th Meridian the humid East meets the arid West.

OFFICIAL STATE MAP: K-16
DAWSON COUNTY

Located: US 30 - downtown Cozad.

Union Pacific passenger train decorated with the American Flag passed the 100th Meridian.

Nebraska State Historical Society

GENERAL CUSTER IN NEBRASKA

General George Armstrong Custer, commanding troops A, D, E, H, K and M of the Seventh Cavalry, camped near here June 22 to 30, 1867, after a march from Fort McPherson, Nebraska. They were campaigning against the elusive Sioux and Cheyenne Indians.

On June 24 Pawnee Killer led a dawn attack on Custer's camp, wounding a sentry. There followed a parley between Custer and his officers and Pawnee Killer, Pole Cat, Fire Lightning and Walks Underground. Neither side was able to learn the plans of the other, and an Indian effort to separate the officers from their command was thwarted. Later Captain Hamilton and forty troopers, pursuing a decoy war party, rode into an ambush seven miles northwest of the camp but fought their way out, killing two warriors.

Custer's supply train of sixteen wagons, returning from Fort Wallace, Kansas, was attacked near Black Butte Creek, Kansas, and killed several Indians. Lt. Kidder, ten troopers and scout Red Bead, carrying orders from Fort Sedgwick, Colorado, missed Custer's camp and were killed near Beaver Creek. Their mutilated bodies were found and buried by Custer on July 12.

The flamboyant career of General Custer ended on the Little Big Horn, Montana, June 25, 1876.

Pawnee Killer, a Sioux leader
Nebraska State Historical Society

Located: US 34 - southern edge of Benkelman.

OFFICIAL STATE MAP: O-11
DUNDY COUNTY

Nebraska State Historical Society

I.P. Olive was a Republican River Rancher in 1876.

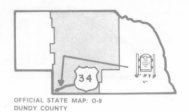

OFFICIAL STATE MAP: O-9
DUNDY COUNTY

Located: US 34 - 4 miles east of Haigler.

NEBRASKA HISTORICAL MARKER

TEXAS TRAIL CANYON

After the slaughter of the buffalo and the last of the Indian hunts, ranchers moved into this part of the Republican River country in 1875. Among them were I. P. and Ira Olive, who were using this canyon on their range in 1876. Herds of Texas cattle were delivered to them here before being driven north to Ogallala.

Prior to 1880, the main Texas-Ogallala Trail entered Nebraska fifty miles east of here, but, with the influx of homesteaders, the trail was pushed west to this area. By 1881 this canyon was known as Texas Trail Canyon, and a checkpoint was established here in 1883-84, where the cattle were checked for brands and disease. It is said that 150,000 cattle were moved through here in 1886, the last year of the trail drives.

A number of pioneer burials were made in the immediate vicinity, beginning with Mexican Leon, a cowboy killed in a fight with Ira Olive. When the railroad built through in 1881-82, a worker was killed and buried 100 yards east of here. Remains of several unidentified pioneers, adults and children, have been discovered over the years, and they were reinterred here in 1971.

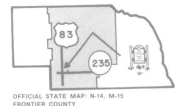

OFFICIAL STATE MAP: N-14, M-15
FRONTIER COUNTY

Two Locations: (1) US 83 - north of McCook and (2) Nebraska 235 - ½ mile west of Stockville.

Nebraska State Historical Society
J.B.Omohundro,"Texas Jack"

NEBRASKA
HISTORICAL MARKER

FRONTIER COUNTY
STOCKVILLE

When Frontier County was organized in 1872, Stockville became the county seat. During its first decade no real town existed, it being only a trading center for the ranchers of the region. It was not until the middle-eighties, when the county filled with homesteaders, that the town began to grow.

Near here is Medicine Creek, one of the most important waterways of the region. It served as a natural highway between the Republican and Platte rivers, first for the Indians, then for the whites. With the establishment of Fort McPherson, the Medicine route was regularly used by the military as they protected the frontier. In the heart of the buffalo country, the Sioux were partial to the Medicine Valley. In 1870, a band of former hostiles--the Whistler band of Cut-off Oglala, settled near here, living in peace with the early settlers for several years.

Among the notable frontiersmen of the region were outstanding figures. Hank and Monty Clifford, John Y. Nelson, and Doc Carver. Regular visitors were Buffalo Bill Cody and Texas Jack Omohundro, as they guided the wealthy on buffalo hunts.

BURTON'S BEND

Faced with the great influx of white settlers after the Civil War, hostile Sioux and Cheyenne Indians retreated into the Republican River Valley. Here they found a nearly ideal location since the valley remained one of the great buffalo ranges of the American West until the 1870's.

Regular military patrols came to the Republican on the Fort McPherson Trail, which followed the divide between Deer and Medicine creeks and entered the valley one mile west. The largest military force to use this route was General Carr's Republican Valley Expedition of 1869. After his successful campaign, the region was clear of hostile Indians.

In 1870 Isaac "Ben" Burton settled one mile southeast on a bend of the Republican at the One Hundredth Meridian. Burton, the first permanent settler of Furnas County, and his partner, H. Dice, established the Burton's Bend Trading Post. This post supplied necessities to the buffalo-hide hunters, who soon killed off the great herd.

For many years the community continued to be known as Burton's Bend, but after the railroad came, its name was changed to Holbrook.

Brevet Major General Eugene A. Carr
Nebraska State Historical Society

Located: US 34 and 6 - Holbrook.

OFFICIAL STATE MAP: N-16
FURNAS COUNTY

Artist's conception of the Norwegian Lutheran Church

OFFICIAL STATE MAP: N-16
FURNAS COUNTY

Located: Northwest of Holbrook, northeast on Deer Creek Lutheran Church grounds.

NEBRASKA HISTORICAL MARKER

NORWEGIAN LUTHERAN CHURCH

Among the first settlers in Southwest Nebraska were a small group of Norwegians, who settled along Deer Creek in Furnas and Gosper counties in 1873. At that time the region was still a part of the buffalo range and a major Indian hunting grounds.

In October 1877, those pioneers met at the home of Erickson Fosse for religious services, and they organized what was to become the Deer Creek Norwegian Evangelical Lutheran Congregation. The charter members were the families of Eric Erickson, Ole Olson, A. E. Phillipson, Ellen Simon, Nels Simon and Ole Simon. Church services were held in the homes of the members until 1888, when Mr. Phillipson donated an acre of land on the west bank of Deer Creek for a church site and cemetery. A small church was erected in 1889. By that time, the church membership also included the Benjamin, Christianson, Hanson, Lee, Madison, Olson, Oswald, Petterson and Thompson families.

By 1902 the membership had outgrown the small church and the present building was started the following year. The new church was dedicated in May 1904.

THE REPUBLICAN RIVER FLOOD OF 1935

On May 30, 1935, torrential rains fell in eastern Colorado and southwestern Nebraska; by early morning of the 31st, the usually peaceful Republican River was running bluff-to-bluff along its upper reaches. When the waters subsided two days later, over 100 lives had been lost and many millions of dollars of damage had been done. A number of persons from this community were drowned.

After the prolonged drouth of the early 30's, the wet spring of 1935 had brought welcome relief to the region. By the end of May, however, the soil was nearing the saturation point. The rains of May 30th, concentrated in the basin of the South Fork and extending into the valleys of the Arikaree, Frenchman, Red Willow, and Medicine, poured into the main stream--normally 300 to 400 feet wide, turning it into a raging torrent one to four miles wide.

The flood water came as a wall, variously estimated at from three to eight feet in height. The advance of the crest was more rapid in the upper valley, reported at ten miles an hour above Trenton, at five between there and Oxford, and slowing to 2½ miles an hour upon crossing over into Kansas.

To prevent the repetition of such a tragedy the federal government has built a series of six dams, five in Nebraska, across the Republican or its tributaries, serving not only as flood protection, but providing recreation and irrigation facilities as well.

OFFICIAL STATE MAP: N-17
FURNAS COUNTY

Located: US 136 - 3 miles west of Oxford.

The Republican River flooded in 1935 swamping Trenton's streets.

Nebraska State Historical Society

Nebraska State Historical Society
Senator Phineas W. Hitchcock

OFFICIAL STATE MAP: G-19
GARFIELD COUNTY

Located: Nebraska 91 - on private property east of Burwell.

NEBRASKA HISTORICAL MARKER

KAMP KALEO

On September 29, 1875, Richard McClimans filed a timber claim on this site under the provisions of the Timber Culture Act of 1873. The original act, sponsored by Senator Phineas W. Hitchcock of Nebraska, enabled homesteaders to acquire up to a quarter section of additional land by agreeing to cultivate timber on the tract.

In 1960, a portion of the McClimans Timber Claim was donated to the Nebraska Conference of the United Church of Christ by the family of Osceola and Laura McClimans Cram, as a memorial in their honor. Named Kamp Kaleo, additional acreage was acquired by the church in 1961, and added to the original donation. Many of the trees on the grounds of Kamp Kaleo are survivors of the original McClimans Timber Claim, and some 32 acres of forest have been designated a managed nature area by the Soil Conservation Society of America.

Although the Timber Culture Act was largely unsuccessful in the promotion of tree planting on the plains, Kamp Kaleo testifies that pioneer farmers often made significant contributions to the natural beauty of Nebraska.

NEBRASKA
HISTORICAL MARKER

CHALK MINE

The fertile North Loup Valley provided food and construction materials for the early settlers of this region. When they came here in 1872 they were greeted by Jack Swearengen, a trapper, guide, and government scout. He lived near here in a dugout in the white chalk bluffs that rise above the valley. The highest hill became known as "Happy Jack's Peak" and served as a lookout-point to guard against surprise Indian attacks.

The hills took on added importance in 1877 when Ed Wright began to mine the chalk. With stone cut from the bluffs, Wright completed construction of a general store in 1887. This building still stands in Scotia, two miles north of here. Other pioneer residents soon began using chalk in the foundations of their buildings.

The mine stood idle for a number of years. It was reopened in the 1930's by a paint company of Omaha. The chalk was used in a variety of ways, not only in paint and whitewash, but also in cement, polishes and chicken feed. These formations of calcarious rock, which can be seen throughout the North Loup Valley, were permanently preserved here in 1967 when the mine area was purchased by the Nebraska State Game and Parks Commission for use as a wayside park.

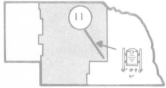

OFFICIAL STATE MAP: I-20
GREELEY COUNTY

Located: Nebraska 11 - southeast of Scotia at state wayside rest.

Loup Valley homesteaders

Nebraska State Historical Society

140

OFFICIAL STATE MAP: N-13
HITCHCOCK COUNTY

Located: US 34 - city park in Culbertson.

Nebraska State Historical Society

W.Z. Taylor

NEBRASKA
HISTORICAL MARKER

CULBERTSON
FIRST HITCHCOCK COUNTY SEAT

Culbertson was the county seat of Hitchcock County for twenty years, and this marks the site of the first court house, used 1886-1893. Founded as a trading post in July 1873 by W. Z. Taylor, it became the county seat when Hitchcock County was organized August 30, 1873. The county was named for U. S. Senator P. W. Hitchcock, and the town was named for Alexander Culbertson, noted fur trader of the Upper Missouri then living at Orleans.

The community consisted of Taylor's store and J. E. Kleven's blacksmith shop and post office until 1875, when thousands of Texas cattle were brought into the four southwest Nebraska counties. Culbertson was the only town in the region, and the ranchers made it their headquarters, many serving as county officials.

During the years of the "open range," the ranchers spent summers on the range, but moved to Culbertson in winter, taking advantage of the schools and social life. The railroad arrived in 1881, and thousand of homesteaders flocked into the county displacing the ranchers. During this period, Culbertson became a pioneer irrigation center. In 1893, the county seat was moved to Trenton, near the center of the county.

NEBRASKA
HISTORICAL MARKER

MASSACRE CANYON

The adjacent stone monument erected in 1930 was first placed about a mile south of this area. Originally on the highway overlooking the canyon, it was moved to this location after the highway was relocated.

Massacre Canyon is the large canyon about half a mile west of here. The battle took place in and along this canyon when a Pawnee hunting party of about 700, confident of protection from the government, were surprised by a War Party of Sioux. The Pawnee, badly outnumbered and completely surprised, retreated into the head of the canyon about two miles northwest of here. The battle was the retreat of the Pawnee down the canyon to the Republican.

The Pawnee reached the Republican River, about a mile and a half south of here, and crossed to the other side. The Sioux were ready to pursue them still further, but a unit of cavalry arrived and prevented further fighting.

The defeat so broke the strength and spirit of the tribe that it moved from its reservation in central Nebraska to Oklahoma.

OFFICIAL STATE MAP: N-12
HITCHCOCK COUNTY

Located: US 34 - east of Trenton.

This is Massacre Canyon with the monument on a hill in the background.

Nebraska State Historical Society

Nebraska State Historical Society

First courthouse, Holt County

Located: US 20 - 2 miles east
of O'Neill.

OFFICIAL STATE MAP: D-20
HOLT COUNTY

NEBRASKA HISTORICAL MARKER

O'NEILL

One of the most colorful leaders in the early development of Nebraska was General John O'Neill, founder of O'Neill. After leading several ill-fated raids against British military posts in Canada, 1866-1871, O'Neill lost his leading position in the Fenians--an American organization promoting Irish independence. Born in Ireland in 1834, he was a U.S. Army officer from 1857 to 1864, when he became active in the Fenians. In 1871, though in disfavor with the leading Irish-American society, O'Neill did not give up the cause.

Thousands of Irish were leaving troubled Ireland to settle in crowded American cities. O'Neill became interested in founding agrarian colonies in the West. For his first colony, he selected Holt County, on Nebraska's frontier. The first colonists arrived in May 1874, and his fourth and last group arrived in 1877. General O'Neill died the following year, but the town was already the county seat and growing.

Though there were numerous Irish settlements in Nebraska, O'Neill was the largest formal Irish colony. Its citizens have always been proud of their Old World Heritage.

O'NEILL
IRISH CAPITAL OF NEBRASKA

The Irish were a major immigrant group contributing to the settlement of Nebraska. Speaking the English language, they blended into the population and were found in many communities. However, due to ancient animosities with Britain, some of them colonized in America. Foremost colony in this State is O'Neill, proclaimed the Irish Capital of Nebraska by the Governor in 1969.

O'Neill, county seat of Holt County, was founded by General John O'Neill, a native of Ireland and veteran of the American Civil War. The "general," a rank bestowed on him by admirers because he commanded three Fenian incursions into British-governed Canada, first directed colonists in 1874 to this fertile Elkhorn Valley site which bears his name. General O'Neill also induced other Irish groups to settle at Atkinson in Holt County and in Greeley County.

Many Irish coming to O'Neill had emigrated to America earlier, as result of famine and economic distress, temporarily settling in eastern cities. General O'Neill, knowing the agricultural heritage of his people, said his object in founding Nebraska colonies was "to encourage poor people in getting away from the overcrowded cities of the East."

OFFICIAL STATE MAP: D-20
HOLT COUNTY

Located: US 20 - 1 block north of stop light at Courthouse green at O'Neill.

Early O'Neill was full of people and activity during Registration.

Nebraska State Historical Society

144

Located: US 275 - eastern
edge of Ewing.

OFFICIAL STATE MAP: E-21
HOLT COUNTY

NEBRASKA
HISTORICAL MARKER

THE SAVIDGE BROTHERS, AVIATION PIONEERS

Near here was the scene of some of Nebraska's earliest experiments with flight in a heavier-than-air vehicle. Sometime before late 1907, Martin P. Savidge's sons set out to construct a flying machine.

They began by studying hawks, then went on to build model gliders, then full size gliders, and finally a self-powered airplane. The first public demonstration was successfully held on Sunday, May 7, 1911.

Following this success, the brothers spent five years barnstorming throughout the Great Plains. Matt Savidge was among the first to develop a method of skywriting. During these five years, the brothers built and flew three different biplanes.

After a barnstorming tour through Texas, the brothers returned home in the spring of 1916 to make repairs and adjustments on their plane. During a test flight on June 17, 1916, the plane crashed, killing Matt Savidge.

After this tragedy, the family of the young fliers insisted that they give up their dangerous pastime. Thus ended one of the earliest chapters of Nebraska aviation history.

ASH HOLLOW
Gateway to the North Platte Valley

Although some wagon trains continued to follow the South Platte, most crossed at one of several fords in this area and took a northwesterly route toward the North Platte River. The trail then followed the North Platte Valley through the remainder of Nebraska. Today's traveler, by following U.S. Highway 28 northwest of Ogallala, will encounter several noted landmarks along this portion of the Platte River Road.

One of these is Ash Hollow, a picturesque canyon, near present-day Lewellen. Because of the steepness of the descent, this part of the trail presented one of the most serious obstacles yet faced by the emigrants. Offering spectacular scenery as well as wood and water, Ash Hollow is mentioned in many overland diaries. Several graves including that of young Rachel Pattison who died of cholera in 1849, testify to the rigors of the overland journey.

Northwest of Ash Hollow on Blue Water Creek was the site of a significant Indian battle in 1855. Often known as the Battle of Ash Hollow, this fight resulted in the defeat of the Little Thunder's band of Brule Sioux by United States Troops under General William S. Harney.

General William Selby Harney

Nebraska State Historical Society

Located: I-80 West - 6 miles east of Ogallala at rest area.

OFFICIAL STATE MAP: J-10
KEITH COUNTY

146

Located: I-80 West - 6 miles
east of Ogallala at rest area.

NEBRASKA
HISTORICAL MARKER

COURT HOUSE ROCK, CHIMNEY ROCK AND SCOTT'S BLUFFS

Traveling northwest from Ash Hollow, the emigrants encountered three natural features of the North Platte Valley which became well-known milestones. First was Court House Rock, rising abruptly from the plains as the vanquard of the bluffs farther on. Observers likened this gigantic formation to some great public building or medieval castle.

However, no single sight along the trail attracted as much attention as Chimney Rock. The tower, which could be seen for miles, served as a beacon for the weary travelers. Many camped nearby, and Chimney Rock is mentioned in more trail accounts than any other landmark. Although the spire is slowly crumbling due to erosion, Chimney Rock remains a unique natural wonder.

As the wagon trains approached the end of their journey across Nebraska, they were greeted by a series of citadel-like eminences, dominated by the imposing bulk of Scott's Bluffs. Named after fur trader Hiram Scott, the Bluffs are now a national monument.

Visible traces of the great migration still survive in some areas, and the landmarks remain for the modern traveler who chooses to follow the route of the Great Platte River Road.

Downey's Midwest Studio, Scottsbluff

Courthouse and Jail House Rocks

COWBOY CAPITAL

Named for the Oglala band of Dakota Sioux and located on the Union Pacific Railroad, Ogallala was a lusty cowtown of the Old West. From 1875 to 1885 it was a wild woolly cowboy capital where gold flowed across the gaming tables, liquor across the bar, and often blood across the floor.

As farmers settled eastern Oklahoma and Kansas, they destroyed the famous Chisholm Trail, forcing the herds westward, and the Western or Texas Trail through Dodge City to Ogallala was established. From Ogallala, Texas cattle were shipped East or sold to ranchers from Nebraska, Montana, Wyoming, Dakota, and Colorado. Indian agencies and mining camps provided an early market for Ogallala beef.

Ogallala, the cowtown, was a lively and colorful segment of the American West and the chief gateway to the newly opened ranges of the northern plains. By 1884 the trail driving days were virtually ended and the Old West and Ogallala turned to other ways of life. Cattle remain an important factor in the area along with farming, hydro-electric power and industry.

OFFICIAL STATE MAP: J-10
KEITH COUNTY

Located: US 30 - Main Street
City Park at Ogallala.

This was a typical scene in a cowboy's life.

Nebraska State Historical Society

Located: US 30 - Park Hill
Drive and West 10th Street
at Ogallala.

OFFICIAL STATE MAP: J-10
KEITH COUNTY

NEBRASKA
HISTORICAL MARKER

BOOT HILL

Boot Hill was the final resting place for many early westerners who helped make Ogallala a booming cowtown in the 1870's and 1880's. These people, the cowboys, settlers, and drifters, came to Ogallala when the railroad and the Texas Trail opened a new market for the Texas Longhorn.

Although one of the first burials here was a mother and child, many came by running afoul of the law -- some for stealing another man's horse. Others were killed by refighting the Civil War or for questioning the gambler's winning hand. In July of 1879 three cowhands were buried in a single day, victims of the sheriff's guns. Another man, "Rattlesnake Ed", was buried here after he was shot down over a nine dollar bet in a Monte game in the Cowboys Rest, a local saloon.

Most were buried with their boots on, thus the name Boot Hill. Their bodies, placed in canvas sacks, were lowered into shallow graves and marked with a wooden headboard. Some of the bodies have since been removed, only the unknown or the unclaimed remain in this western cemetery.

Nebraska State Historical Society

This is Front Street of recreated early Ogallala.

Early Ogallala

Nebraska State Historical Society

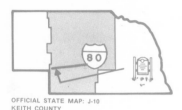

OFFICIAL STATE MAP: J-10
KEITH COUNTY

Located: I-80 West - 6 miles
east of Ogallala at rest area.

NEBRASKA
HISTORICAL MARKER

OGALLALA AND THE PLATTE VALLEY

This region holds much that is significant to the history of the West. At this point, I-80 follows the route of the Overland Trail, along the South Platte River. Leaving the South Platte near here, the trail continued up the North Platte Valley, today the route of U.S. 26. Beginning in 1841, an estimated quarter of a million travelers crossed the plains over this great natural highway. Oregon and California were early goals, and the Platte Valley later became an important freighting and military route. The Pony Express used the Platte River Road, and when the first trans-continental railroad was completed in 1869, it too followed the valley.

Nearby Ogallala was a wild and woolly cowtown from 1875 to 1885 while the northern terminus of the Texas Trail. Located on the Union Pacific Railroad, the town was a shipping point for great herds of Texas Longhorns, and the chief gateway to the newly opened ranges of the Northern Plains. Boot Hill, which still survives, was the final resting place for many who helped make Ogallala the Cowboy Capital of Nebraska.

Buffalo Bill Ranch
State Historical Park

STATE HISTORICAL PARK

Another famous Nebraska house belonged to the legendary William F. "Buffalo Bill" Cody at North Platte. There, Cody wintered after touring with his famous Wild West Show. Buffalo Bill Ranch State Historical Park tells the story of this colorful man who took the wild west to the world. His exloits before his stage career are well documented, including his stints as a Pony Express rider and as a scout for the military. Both the house and barn are filled with Cody memorabilia, and a log cabin that he used during his ranching days on the Dismal River is also standing on the park grounds.

Buffalo Bill, noted frontier scout, originator of rodeo, and one of the West's greatest salesmen, headquartered his world-famous congress of rough riders at his ranch near North Platte.

Nebraska Game and Parks Commission

Located: I-80 at western edge of North Platte, turn west on Nebraska 30 at Buffalo Bill Avenue.

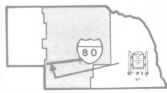

OFFICIAL STATE MAP: J-13
LINCOLN COUNTY

151

STATE
HISTORICAL
PARK

Nebraska Game and Parks Commission

Scouts Rest Ranch, home of the famous William F. (Buffalo Bill) Cody, is near North Platte. Now a state historical park, the ranch features the restored ranch house, the famous wine cellar, and the huge barn where Bill's wild west show troop wintered and rehearsed.

STATE
HISTORICAL
PARK

Although Buffalo Bill's ranch was called "Scouts Rest" the ranch was a working 7,000-acre cattle ranch. Scouts Rest was also the home base for the Wild West Show. Typical of the ranch house is this sample of the dining room wallpaper.

Nebraska Game and Parks Commission

Nebraska Game and Parks Commission

The Cody big red barn could be seen miles away by Union Pacific Railroad passengers. The barn has outside rafters shaped like gunstocks.

This is the cabin Buffalo Bill lived in when he ranched near Dismal River.

Nebraska Game and Parks Commission

Located: I-80 East - Sutherland Rest Area.

NEBRASKA
HISTORICAL MARKER

CROSSING THE OVERLAND TRAIL

Beneath this platform, evidence of the great westward migration still remains. These shallow depressions were once deep ruts created by thousands of hooves, shoes and wheels. The Overland Trail is often visualized as a single, well-defined roadway. However, except in narrow spots such as this, the actual route through the Platte Valley during any given year varied considerably, depending upon such factors as soil conditions and the availability of grass for the animals. Traveling an average of fifteen to twenty miles a day in various conveyances, the emigrants spent from four to six months on the trail during the long trek from the Missouri River to Oregon or California. At best, the journey was arduous, often marked only by the dusty monotony of daily routine. At other times, disease and Indian attacks were very real dangers, and the number of fresh graves along the road bore testimony to the sacrifices made by many pioneers. Some emigrants were better equipped than others, some were wiser, some were simply luckier; but all suffered weariness, hardship and danger. However, as the many overland diaries and letters testify, this was a great human experience, one which was vital to the settlement of the West.

Nebraska State Historical Society

This woodcut was first printed in 1836.

FORT MCPHERSON

The fort was established on the Oregon Trail on the south side of the Platte River in October 1863, on the eve of intensified Indian raids on the Plains. Built next to the well-known Cottonwood Springs and McDonald ranche, it commanded a strategic north-south Indian trail across the Platte valley.

First known as Cantonment McKean and then Fort Cottonwood, in February 1886 the fort was named for Major-General James B. McPherson. It served to protect the important Platte valley line of travel and communication and was the base for innumerable scouting parties and for field campaigns in 1865, 1866 and 1869. General Carr's campaign in 1869 broke the power of the Cheyennes and cleared the surrounding area from more than temporary Indian threats.

The Russian Grand Duke Alexis prepared here for his famous buffalo hunt in 1872. General Custer, Buffalo Bill, the North Brothers and their Pawnee scouts were often at the Fort.

The fort was abandoned in 1880, but a portion of the military reservation is now the Fort McPherson National Cemetery where rest soldiers from McPherson and other frontier forts.

Major General McPherson

Nebraska State Historical Society

Located: US 30 - west of Maxwell.

OFFICIAL STATE MAP: J-14
LINCOLN COUNTY

Two Locations: (1) I-80 West - Sutherland Rest Area, and (2) I-80 East - Sutherland Rest Area.

NEBRASKA
HISTORICAL MARKER

THE GREAT PLATTE RIVER ROAD

This is the Platte River Valley, America's great road west. It provided a natural pathway for westward expansion across the continent during the nineteenth century. Here passed the Oregon Trail, following the South Platte River along much the same route as the highway over which you now travel. Beginning in 1841, nearly 250,000 travelers crossed the plains to Oregon and California over this important overland route. Here at O'Fallon's Bluffs, the wagon trains faced one of the most difficult and dangerous spots on the trail. The Platte River cut directly against the bluff, making it necessary to travel the narrow roadway over O'Fallon's Bluffs. Deep sand caught the wagon wheels, and Indian attacks were always a danger. A few feet southeast of this point, ruts made by thousands of wagon wheels still remain.

Although first traveled primarily by immigrants, the trail was later used by the Pony Express and became an important freight and military route. With the completion of the trans-continental railroad across Nebraska in 1867, travel on the trail declined. Although the dangers and hardships faced by early travelers no longer exist, the Great Platte Valley route remains an important modern thoroughfare across Nebraska and across the nation.

Nebraska State Historical Society

Early pony express station placed in Nebraska

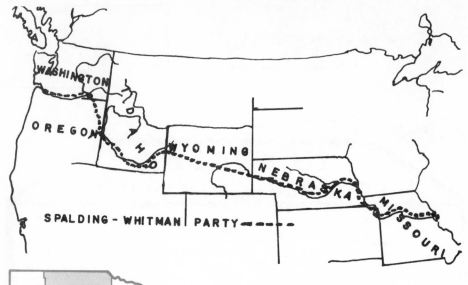

Located: I-80 - southeast of
North Platte at Sioux Lookout
Hill.

OFFICIAL STATE MAP: J-13
LINCOLN COUNTY

NEBRASKA
HISTORICAL MARKER

SIOUX LOOKOUT

Sioux Lookout, the highest point in Lincoln County, was a prominent landmark on the overland trails. From its lofty summit the development of the West unfolded before the eyes of the Sioux and other Indians. Trappers and traders came by here in 1813, the first wagon train in 1830, and the first missionary in 1834. In 1836 Narcissa Whitman and Elizabeth Spalding became the first white women to travel the trail. During the Indian War of 1864-1865, its prominence gave a clear view of troop and Indian movements below.

Gold seekers enroute to California, homesteaders seeking freeland in the West and a religious people seeking a haven in Utah--all are part of the history of this valley. Here echoed the hooves of the Pony Express. From 1840 to 1866 some 2,500,000 people traveled the valley, engraving into the sod a wide, deep trail. Indians called the route "The Great Medicine Road of the Whites."

In 1869 the transcontinental railroad was completed, ending much of the trail travel. Yet even today, the valley with its ribbons of concrete remains the Great Platte River Road to the West.

Located: Nebraska 23 -
eastern edge of Madrid.

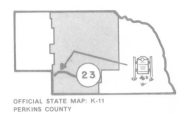

OFFICIAL STATE MAP: K-11
PERKINS COUNTY

NEBRASKA
HISTORICAL MARKER

THE TEXAS TRAIL

After the Civil War, herds of Texas cattle were driven north to marketing points in eastern Nebraska, but settlement by homesteaders forced the trail further west each year. Beginning in 1875, Union Pacific selected Ogallala as its main shipping point. During the following decade, thousands of longhorn cattle were trailed through Perkins County, in the vicinity of this marker.

Beginning in Texas the trail turned northward through the Indian Territory into western Kansas. From Dodge City on the Arkansas River, the trail continued to Buffalo Station, Kansas, entering Nebraska in Hitchcock County. The hardest day's drive for the trail-weary men and cattle was the 30 miles from the head of Stinking Water Creek in southeast Perkins County to Ogallala on the South Platte; it was the longest and driest drive of the trip.

In 1876 over 60,000 Texas cattle were driven over the trail, and between 1879 and 1884 over 100,000 cattle made the trip each year, with the last great drive occuring in 1884. Due to settlement in the counties to the south, as well as in Perkins County, the last drives were made through the western part of the county.

Nebraska State Historical Society

Cattle on the trail

NEBRASKA
HISTORICAL MARKER

WILD HORSE SPRING

Named for the beautiful, spirited wild horses so numerous in this area when white men first visited these lush plains, this Spring symbolizes the hope and faith its discovery brought to the early pioneers. Though the rich land beckoned them, men seeking homesteads had been reluctant to settle this land, so strange and forbidding because of its lack of known water sources.

In the early days this Spring served to quench the thirst of the wild horses, buffalo and other wild animals of the region. Later, its clear, cool waters refreshed the hot and thirsty cowboy, trail weary from the long trek between Stinking Water Creek and the Platte River.

It was never an abundant source of water but it was sufficient to supply the needs of the early settlers until they could dig wells for themselves. The precious, lifegiving water from this Spring, so far from any stream, provided comfort and courage to the men and women who established their homes in this part of the frontier, and it is to them that this marker is dedicated.

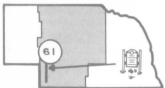

OFFICIAL STATE MAP: K-10
PERKINS COUNTY

Located: Nebraska 61 - north of Grant in a valley.

Nebraska State Historical Society

The Norris Home

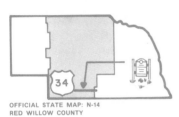

OFFICIAL STATE MAP: N-14
RED WILLOW COUNTY

Located: US 34 - Norris Park
on Main Street at McCook.

Nebraska State Historical Society

George William Norris

NEBRASKA
HISTORICAL MARKER

GEORGE WILLIAM NORRIS
1861-1944

George W. Norris, whose home is on Norris Avenue, McCook, Nebraska, served forty years in the Congress of the United States. Born in Ohio, he worked his way through college, followed the footsteps of the pioneers westward, settling in Nebraska. He began his public career as County Attorney of Furnas County, served as District Judge for seven years, was elected in 1902 to the first of five consecutive terms in the United States House of Representatives.

Elected to the United States Senate in 1912, beginning a service of thirty years, he championed the rights of the common man, and the conservation and development of our natural resources for the benefit of all. Among his great achievements are the Tennessee Valley Authority, the Rural Electrification Administration, the Twentieth Amendment to the Constitution of the United States, and the Anti-Injunction Act, as well as the establishment of the Unicameral Legislature in the State of Nebraska. He was elected to the Nebraska Hall of Fame in 1961.

George W. Norris, the "Gentle Knight of Progressive Ideals", one of the Nation's great statesmen, served well the State and the Nation.

MALLALIEU UNIVERSITY

In June, 1886, the townsite of Bartley was platted on land owned by the Reverend Allen Bartley, a minister of the Methodist Church. The previous year, Methodist Bishop Mallalieu had proposed this site as the location for a church-affiliated institution of higher education, and in April, 1886, the Reverend Bartley was authorized to establish a University here. By July, some 27 buildings had been erected in the new town.

The University, named for Bishop Mallalieu, was opened in September, 1886, with an enrollment of sixty students. Courses were taught in the liberal arts, music, and business. The first class was graduated in the spring of 1888, and that summer, construction began on the first of the permanent University buildings, Haddock Hall, which was located a short distance north of this point.

The Hall was not completed however, as drought and adverse economic conditions soon forced the University to close its doors. The school never reopened, and the bricks from Haddock Hall were later used in the construction of the Methodist Church of Bartley, the only reminder of this early attempt to bring higher education to southwest Nebraska.

OFFICIAL STATE MAP: N-15
RED WILLOW COUNTY

Located: US 34 - Bartley Town Park.

Sod Schoolhouse, Bartley

Nebraska State Historical Society

Nebraska State Historical Society

"Prairie Fire" sketch

Located: US 20 - ½ mile west
of Newport.

OFFICIAL STATE MAP: D-18
ROCK COUNTY

NEBRASKA
HISTORICAL MARKER

SPRING VALLEY PARK

Welcome to Spring Valley Park. Pioneers of this region, eastern Rock County, recognized it as a great natural haying region extending over twenty miles south down this valley. The nearby village of Newport, established in 1883, became one of the major hay shipping centers in the nation, with thousands of tons being exported each year. Prairie fires have been a major threat to farmers and ranchers. The great prairie fire of 1904 burned over forty miles northward through the county, causing major damage to farmsteads, crops and livestock, and the village of Newport was threatened with destruction.

Because of the fine pasturage, Rock County developed into a major beef producing region, sending thousands of cattle annually to livestock marketing centers. Travelers through the area can view the herds of prime beef cattle.

On this site about 1938, Vic and Maude Thompson established what is considered to be the first roadside rest area in Nebraska. Over the years it has provided comfort to thousands of travelers, and in 1966 they dedicated this Centennial Memorial Forest and proclaimed their ranch a wild life refuge, free to all. For Safety's Sake...Stop and Rest.

163

NEBRASKA
HISTORICAL MARKER

THE SANDHILLS

The Sandhills, Nebraska's most unique physiographic feature, cover about one-fourth of the state. The sandy soil acts like a giant sponge, soaking up rain and forming a vast underground reservoir. Hundreds of permanent lakes are found here. However, the same sandy soil makes the area unsuitable for cultivation. Grasses flourish, making the Sandhills ideal cattle country.

Although the Sandhills were long considered "an irreclaimable desert," cattlemen had begun to discover the Sandhills' potential as range land by the early 1870's. Huge ranches were established here.

Unsuccessful attempts at farming were made in the Sandhills region in the late 1870's and again around 1890. The Kinkaid Act of 1904 allowed homesteaders to claim a full section of land, rather than the quarter-section previously allowed. Nearly nine million acres were successfully claimed by "Kinkaiders" between 1910 and 1917. Some of the Kinkaiders attempted to farm, but most of these attempts failed. Many of the largest ranches broke up about the same time due to regulations against fencing federal range. Today the Sandhills contain many ranches, but none so large as those of the past.

OFFICIAL STATE MAP: F-14
THOMAS COUNTY

Located: Intersection Nebraska 83 and 2 - 1½ miles east of Thedford.

The Sandhills, cattle country

Nebraska State Historical Society

OFFICIAL STATE MAP: H-19
VALLEY COUNTY

Located: Nebraska 11 - ¼ mile south of Elyria.

STATE HISTORICAL PARK

NEBRASKA
HISTORICAL MARKER

FORT HARTSUFF 1874-1881

The North Loup Valley provided a route for the Sioux raids upon the Pawnee. In 1872 white settlers moved into the valley. Sioux depredations at Sioux Creek in October 1873 and at Pebble Creek in January of 1874 prompted the settlers to request military protection.

The fort, originally designated as "Post on the North Fork of the Loup River," was established on September 5, 1874. On December 9, 1874, the post was renamed in honor of Major General George L. Hartsuff.

Fort Hartsuff became the center of the social life of the valley, and through disbursement of supplies, helped to offset the effects of the drought and grasshopper invasions of the early 1870's. The fort's major military engagement came at the Battle of the Blow Out in April of 1876. The action resulted in the death of First Sergeant Dougherty when troops commanded by Lieutenant Heyl routed a band of hostile Sioux.

By 1881 the railroad was extended into the valley, an orderly civilian government had been established and the threat of hostilities was ended. Fort Hartsuff was abandoned on May 1, 1881. Today it is a State Historical Park.

Nebraska State Historical Society

Fort Hartsuff was built in 1874-75.

Fort Hartsuff
State Historical Park

Fort Hartsuff came into being as a result of confrontations between the Indians (mostly Teton Sioux) and white settlers in the North Loup Valley in the early 1870's.

After the "War Between the States", homesteaders streamed into the area eager to stake their claims to free government land. As more and more settlers arrived, they encroached farther and farther into lands the Indians had traditionally roamed at will. One skirmish between the Indians and Whites in 1873 on Sioux Creek, 15 miles west of this site, resulted in a loss of $1,500 worth of horses. A year later, Marion Littlefield of Clay County was killed by the Indians at Pebble Creek near the fork of the Loup and Calamus Rivers.

A fort on the North Loup was needed not only to protect the white settlers, but the friendly Pawnee as well. The Pawnee reservation near Genoa was subject to raids by their traditional enemies, the nomadic Sioux. Another factor was the abandonment of Fort Kearny on the Platte River to the south.

General O. E. C. Ord, famed Civil War soldier, led the detachment that selected the site for the new fort. Construction began in the fall of 1874 and cost $110,000. The nine major buildings at Fort Hartsuff were constructed of concrete, since ample supplies of gravel were available locally. This factor contributed greatly to the ability of the structures to survive the passage of time. Four of the original buildings have been renovated—the adjutant's office, officers' quarters, hospital, and guardhouse. The five others are being stabilized and represent their natural condition after years of use.

Named for Major General George L. Hartsuff, another Civil War hero, the post served as a rallying point for Loup Valley settlers during its seven years as an active military installation. Dances, Fourth of July celebrations, and other gala occasions drew settlers from 30 miles around and particularly from the settlement fringes to the west. The fort was considered the most pleasant duty station in the entire Department of the Platte.

1946 aerial photo of Fort Hartsuff

Nebraska State Historical Society

The years 1873-75 were bitterly hard for settlers in the area, what with drought, grasshoppers, and depression. Consequently, employment opportunities at Fort Hartsuff drew workers from as far away as the South Loup and Platte River valleys. Wages were good, for a man with a team of horses could earn $3 a day.

Strength of the garrison was never large, generally one infantry company of less than 100 men. During the life of the fort, the 9th, 14th, and 23rd Infantry were stationed there. Primary duties included scouting the Loup and Cedar rivers for hostile Sioux, often traveling as far north as the Niobrara River. Other duties included aiding civil authorities in pursuit of horse thieves, murderers, and train robbers. In 1877, a detachment was detailed to escort travelers to Deadwood in the Black Hills to pioneer a new trail from Grand Island to the gold fields.

The major encounter with the Sioux occurred in April, 1876, a few miles northwest of the present town of Burwell and came to be known as the "Battle of the Blowout". A party of braves was harassing the settlers and a detachment from Company A, 23rd Infantry, was sent out from the fort. The ensuing conflict resulted in the death of Sgt. William Dougherty. Three of the soldiers received the Congressional Medal of Honor for gallantry—2nd Lt. Charles Heath Heyl, Cpl. Patrick Leonard, and Cpl. Jeptha L. Lytton. Ironically, Sgt. Dougherty did not receive the Medal of Honor posthumously. He had already received the medal for bravery in action against the Indians in Arizona in 1868.

In 1880, the Army decided to abandon the post. It had served its purpose. Settlement proceeded rapidly, the Pawnee had been moved to Oklahoma, and the power of the Sioux was broken. Orders for abandonment were issued by the Department of the Platte on April 13, 1881.

Fort Hartsuff was subsequently sold to the Union Pacific Railroad for $5,000. When the railroad decided not to build a line up the north side of the Loup River it was sold into private hands and farmed. In 1961, Dr. Glen Auble of Ord presented the site to the State of Nebraska for preservation and interpretation by the Game and Parks Commission as an historical park.

Nebraska Game and Parks Commission **Blacksmith Shop, Fort Hartsuff**

STATE
HISTORICAL
PARK

Officers' Quarters

Nebraska Game and Parks Commission

Barracks, dining-room, kitchen at Fort Hartsuff

Nebraska State Historical Society

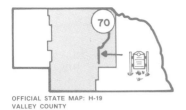

OFFICIAL STATE MAP: H-19
VALLEY COUNTY

Located: Nebraska 70 - 9
miles south of Ord.

Nebraska State Historical Society   Minnie Freeman

NEBRASKA HISTORICAL MARKER

THE BLIZZARD OF 1888

On January 12, 1888, a sudden fierce blizzard slashed across the Midwest. The temperature fell to between 30 and 40 degrees below zero. A howling northwest wind swept the plains. The storm raged for 12 to 18 hours and is probably the most severe single blizzard to have hit Nebraska since the settlement of the state.

Sometimes called "the school children's storm," the blizzard caught many children away from home. Many acts of heroism were performed by parents, teachers, and the children themselves.

The story of Minnie Freeman has become symbolic of these many acts of heroism. Miss Freeman, still in her teens at the time, was teaching at a school near here. When the wind tore the roof off the sod schoolhouse, Miss Freeman saved her pupils by leading them through the storm to a farmhouse a half mile away.

Many other teachers performed similar acts of heroism, and at least one lost her life in the attempt. No accurate count of the total deaths from the storm is possible, but estimates for Nebraska have ranged from 40 to 100.

Located: Nebraska 70 - Ord Airport.

Nebraska State Historical Society

Ord's first airmail flight was on May 19, 1938. It was piloted by Evelyn Sharp, the nation's youngest pilot, aviatrix.

NEBRASKA
HISTORICAL MARKER

EVELYN SHARP

Evelyn Genevieve Sharp was Nebraska's best-known aviatrix during her eight-year career. She was the daughter of Mr. and Mrs. John E. Sharp and was born October 1, 1919, in Melstone, Montana. Her family moved to Ord in her youth. She became interested in flying at age fourteen, and she soloed under the tutelage of Jack Jefford at sixteen. Two years later she received her commercial pilot's license, one of the youngest persons to achieve this rating. Ord businessmen assisted in the purchase of her first airplane, and she repaid them with profits from barnstorming trips.

At twenty Evelyn became an instructor. Over 350 men learned flying from her in Spearfish, South Dakota, her first teaching assignment. She was the nation's first female airmail pilot. With the coming of World War II, Evelyn joined General H. H. "Hap" Arnold's Women's Auxiliary Ferrying Squadron, expert pilots who flew aircraft from factory sites to shipping points. Her proficiency enabled her to fly everything from training craft to bombers.

On April 3, 1944, at the age of twenty-four, Evelyn Sharp was killed near Middleton, Pennsylvania, in the crash of a P-38 pursuit plane. At the time of her death she was a squadron commander only three flights from her fifth rating, the highest certificate then available to women. She is buried in Ord.

NEBRASKA
HISTORICAL MARKER

NEBRASKA'S
PANHANDLE

NEBRASKA
HISTORICAL MARKER

BOX BUTTE COUNTRY

A flat-topped hill to the southeast was named Box Butte by early cowboys and travellers. This area is part of the Box Butte Tableland, semi-arid short grass country that stretches far to the west.

Box Butte has given its name to the creek that flows near its base, a village, and the county where it is located. It served as a landmark for miners and freighters to the Black Hills during the gold rush of the 1870's. Box Butte City was founded east of here in the mid-1880's. A cluster of sod and frame buildings housed a post office, grocery and drug store, land locator's office, livery barn, hotel, restaurant, two blacksmith shops, and a cream station. A small sod church was built west of the village. The town died when the post office was discontinued in 1910 and only the pioneer graves remain.

Box Butte County was created in 1886 from lands in Dawes County. Heavy advertising campaigns by the railroads spurred its early growth. The Kinkaid Act of 1904 increased the size of homesteads from 160 to 640 acres and aided in the economic recovery of the county following the depression and drought of the 1890's. The landmark remains as a rugged memorial to those hardy pioneers who settled "Box Butte Country."

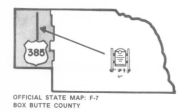

OFFICIAL STATE MAP: F-7
BOX BUTTE COUNTY

Located: US 385 - 16 miles north of Alliance.

Sodhouse, Box Butte County

Nebraska State Historical Society

172

Located: US 385 - 3 miles south of Gurley.

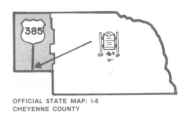

OFFICIAL STATE MAP: I-6
CHEYENNE COUNTY

NEBRASKA
HISTORICAL MARKER

DISCOVERY OIL WELL-MARATHON OIL COMPANY

On August 9, 1949, the first successful oil well in western Nebraska came in for 225 barrels of oil per day at a total depth of 4,429 feet. Marathon Oil Co. completed the discovery well, Mary Egging #1, located four miles east and two miles north of this marker, and five miles southeast of the town of Gurley.

The oil discovery ended 60 years of unsuccessful searching in western Nebraska. The first reported interest for oil occurred in 1889, near Crawford, in the northwest corner of the Panhandle. The first recorded drilling operation took place in 1903 near Chadron, also in the northern part of the Panhandle. In 1917, the first exploratory well to drill in the southwest Panhandle, near Harrisburg, failed. Oil searchers sunk many other dry test wells in western Nebraska until success came in 1949. Wells in the Nebraska Panhandle through 1966 had produced more than 216 million barrels of oil. Nebraska's first successful oil well was completed in 1939 in the southeastern corner of the state.

The first reported interest for oil occurred near Crawford, Dawes County.
Nebraska State Historical Society

Nebraska State Historical Society

Chief Dull Knife refused to lead his Cheyenne people back to Oklahoma.

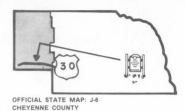

Located: US 30 - eastern edge of Sidney.

NEBRASKA
HISTORICAL MARKER

FORT SIDNEY

Sidney Barracks, when established in 1867, was a temporary camp with one permanent structure, a blockhouse located to the north. In 1869 the Fort was relocated at this site and in 1870 the name was officially changed to Fort Sidney. The primary service of the Fort was in protecting construction crews from hostile Indians while building the Union Pacific.

Fort Sidney became a major strategic point on the Plains in the mid-1870's. With the discovery of gold in the Black Hills, the town of Sidney and the Fort became the major supply point. The trail to Fort Robinson and the Black Hills was of strategic importance during the Indian troubles of 1874-1877 in serving freight wagons and stage coaches. At the same time, Sidney was an important trail town and railhead in the picturesque cattle business of the Old West.

The last Indian alarm at Fort Sidney was the most dramatic. In 1878 the Cheyenne, under Dull Knife, broke from their reservation in Oklahoma and staged an epic flight across Kansas and Nebraska. A special train was kept ready at Sidney to be rushed either way to intercept the Indians when they came to the Union Pacific. On October 4 the train was rushed to Ogallala, but the Indians escaped into the sandhills. The post closed in 1894 and the buildings were sold in 1899.

Located: US 30 - western edge of Sidney.

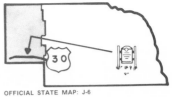

NEBRASKA
HISTORICAL MARKER

SIDNEY - BLACK HILLS TRAIL

Gold was discovered in the Black Hills in August, 1874. By the spring of 1876, the Army had stopped enforcing a treaty which reserved the hills for the Sioux Indians. Miners soon began to pour into the gold regions.

From 1875 to 1881, the 267-mile trail north from Sidney carried the bulk of the traffic to the mining towns of Deadwood and Custer. The Union Pacific Railroad brought men and supplies into Sidney. North from Sidney moved stage coaches, freight wagons drawn by oxen or mules, herds of cattle, and riders on horseback. During 1878-1879 alone, over 22 million pounds of freight moved over the Sidney-Black Hills Trail. Gold shipments, worth up to $200,000 each, moved south from the Black Hills to Sidney and the railroad.

The trail's only major obstacle was the North Platte River. In the spring of 1876, a 2000-foot wooden toll-bridge, known as Clarke's Bridge, was constructed near the present town of Bridgeport.

In October, 1880, the railroad reached Pierre, Dakota Territory, and most of the traffic to the Black Hills was diverted away from Sidney.

Sidney, 1876

Nebraska State Historical Society

175

Union Pacific track layers in Nebraska

Nebraska State Historical Society

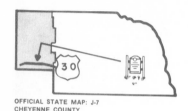

OFFICIAL STATE MAP: J-7
CHEYENNE COUNTY

Located: At depot in Lodgepole.

NEBRASKA
HISTORICAL MARKER

LODGEPOLE AND THE UNION PACIFIC RAILROAD

The history of Lodgepole has been closely associated with railroad development and overland travel in western Nebraska. It was originally established as a station when the Union Pacific Railroad was completed to this point in 1867. A company of U.S. soldiers from nearby Sidney Barracks camped here to guard the railroad against Indian attack, and during the early 1860's a Pony Express station was located a few miles to the east.

Lodgepole derives its name from Lodgepole Creek where Indians reportedly secured timber for their tipi poles. Little permanent settlement occurred until the early 1880's, and the town was platted in 1884. By 1886 it had a population of about 200 people. Stock raising was an important early industry, and many of the state's pioneer ranches were located in the region.

This depot was constructed by the Union Pacific Railroad in 1887 on a site adjacent to the tracks. It replaced an earlier section house and was in use until 1968. In 1971 a gift from Mrs. Doris Bates Rowan in memory of her parents, Mr. and Mrs. B. J. Bates, made possible its preservation at this location, where it now serves as the Lodgepole Depot Museum.

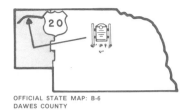

OFFICIAL STATE MAP: B-6
DAWES COUNTY

Located: US 20 - 3 miles east
of Chadron.

Nebraska State Historical Society   James Bordeaux

NEBRASKA
HISTORICAL MARKER

BORDEAUX TRADING POST

From about 1846 until 1872, an Indian "trading house" occupied a site near here. Built by James Bordeaux, the trading station was once attacked and set afire by hostile Crow warriors. Fortunately, some friendly Sioux Indians came to the rescue and drove off the attacking Crow.

James Bordeaux was from a French settlement near St. Louis and while yet a young boy, he went west with fur traders. Bordeaux was active in the fur trade in the vicinity of Fort Laramie from the 1830's until the 1870's. In the 1840's, he served as host to the explorer John C. Fremont and the historian Francis Parkman. He left his name to Bordeaux Bend near Fort Laramie, scene of the Grattan Massacre. His name also survives in the name of Bordeaux Creek, near this marker.

The Indians brought buffalo robes, furs, and ponies to this post to trade for guns, powder, beads, blankets, and whiskey. Some of the weapons may have been used against the troops at Fort Phil Kearny and Custer's troops at the Little Big Horn. The story of James Bordeaux's life is the story of the Upper Missouri country from the 1830's-1870's.

BUTTE COUNTRY

Perhaps no spot in Nebraska is so surrounded by historical and geographical landmarks as this one. Numerous landmarks of the period of the Indian Wars are visible from here. The site of a legendary battle between the Sioux and Crow Indians, Crow Butte, lies directly to the south. It was a pioneer landmark for Indians, soldiers, and cattlemen.

To the west are the Red Cloud Buttes. From these well known buttes, one may see the town of Crawford to the east, Fort Robinson to the south, and the site of the Red Cloud Agency to the southeast. The escarpment stretching north from the buttes was also a prominent early landmark.

Approximately half a mile northwest of this point is the site of the Treaty Tree. There in September, 1875, while thousands of members of the Sioux Indian Nation looked on, the Allison Commission made an unsuccessful attempt to buy the Black Hills area from the Indians. It was not until after the bloody campaigns of 1876 that the Sioux Commission, headed by George Manypenny, succeeded in purchasing the area.

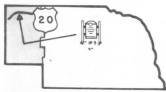

OFFICIAL STATE MAP: C-5
DAWES COUNTY

Located: US 20 - between Chadron and Crawford, east of Crawford.

Located: US 20 - on campus
green at Chadron.

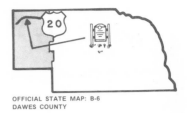

NEBRASKA
HISTORICAL MARKER

CHADRON STATE COLLEGE

Chadron was selected as the site of the fourth Nebraska State Normal School on January 8, 1910, and located on the grounds of the former Chadron Congregational Academy. Classes began in the summer of 1911, concluding with the dedication of the Administration Building. In September, 248 students registered.

By law in 1921, the Normal Schools became Teachers Colleges with the authority to confer the Baccalaureate Degree in Education. The Bachelor of Arts degree was authorized in 1949, and the Master of Science of Education degree in 1955. Recognized as "Nebraska's Pioneering College" for its innovative approaches in Teacher Education, the college has received many national awards.

From its modest beginning, Chadron State College evolved to a rapidly growing multi-purpose institution by mid-century. During the 1960's the college tripled in size. By 1971 the college had achieved an enrollment of 2,469, with nineteen buildings including academic structures and housing complexes located on 213 acres in the "beautiful Nebraska Pine Ridge area." Its Alumni have achieved many honors in other areas as well as education.

Nebraska State Historical Society

First graduating class of Chadron Academy

Chadron State Park   Nebraska State Historical Society

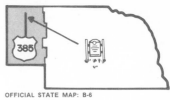

OFFICIAL STATE MAP: B-6
DAWES COUNTY

Located: US 385 - 7 miles south of intersection of Nebraska 20 and US 385 at state park west of Chadron.

NEBRASKA
HISTORICAL MARKER

CHADRON STATE PARK

In 1921 the Nebraska State Legislature created a State Park Board within the Department of Public Works. In 1923, the law was amended by attaching the Board to the Department of Horticulture of the University of Nebraska. The Legislature of 1929 replaced the State Park Board and the Bureau of Game and Fish with a new agency, the Game, Forestation and Parks Commission. In 1967, it was designated by the Legislature as the State Game and Parks Commission.

Chadron State Park was established by a legislative act approved April 25, 1921 and introduced by Senator James Good and Representative George Snow, both of Chadron. This act set aside a section of school land as the first Nebraska State Park. Fifty years later, in 1971, the Parks System had expanded to 93 areas. The Chadron area was once the scene of bitter warfare between the fierce migratory plains Indians and the whites. Later the region was the center of disputes between ranchers and homesteaders who competed for the land from which the Indians had been dispossessed. Today, Chadron, along with other State Parks, provides excellent scenic and recreational areas for the visitor.

OFFICIAL STATE MAP: C-5
DAWES COUNTY

Located: US 20 - the parade grounds of Fort Robinson.

Nebraska State Historical Society

Lt. Levi H. Robinson

NEBRASKA
HISTORICAL MARKER

FORT ROBINSON

In March, 1874, the U.S. Government authorized the establishment of a military camp at the Red Cloud Indian Agency on the White River. Home of some 13,000 Indians, many of whom were hostile, the Agency was one of the most troublesome spots on the Plains. The camp was named Camp Robinson in honor of Lt. Levi H. Robinson, who had been killed by Indians the previous month. In May, the camp was re-located on this site, and in January, 1878, was officially designated Fort Robinson.

Fort Robinson played an important role in the Indian wars from 1876 to 1890. Crazy Horse surrendered here on May 6, 1877, and was mortally wounded that September while resisting imprisonment. In January, 1879, the Fort was the scene of a major battle as the result of the Cheyenne Outbreak led by Chief Dull Knife.

In the 20th Century, Fort Robinson became the world's largest military remount depot, and during the second World War, was the site of a K-9 corps training center, and German prisoner-of-war camp. The Fort's deactivation following the war, marked the end of more than 70 years of service as Nebraska's "outpost on the plains."

Nebraska State Historical Society

Adobe duplex, Fort Robinson

RED CLOUD AGENCY

Red Cloud Agency was established here in 1873 for Chief Red Cloud and his Oglala band, as well as for other northern plains Indians, totaling nearly 13,000. Their earlier agency had been located on the North Platte near Fort Laramie. The agencies served as issuing points for supplies to the Sioux, Cheyenne and Arapaho, authorized in exchange for land ceded to the U.S. in 1868. Dr. J. J. Saville, nominated by the Episcopal Church, was appointed the first agent.

A faction of Agency Indians, joined with visiting hostiles, harassed Saville and his thirty to forty employees, threatened cowboys, and rode through the unfinished stockade shooting out windows. After the establishment of nearby Camp Robinson in March 1874, the agency remained a powder keg. In October 1874, for example, hostiles chopped down the new agency flagpole and threatened to destroy both the agency and the military camp.

During the Indian war of 1876, the agency served as the center for non-hostiles. After the treaty ceding the Black Hills to the U.S. was signed here in 1876, and the death of Crazy Horse in 1877, the agency was relocated to the Pine Ridge Agency, Dakota Territory.

Chief Red Cloud   Nebraska State Historical Society

Located: US 20 - hilltop on agency grounds east of Fort Robinson.

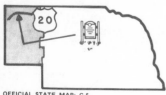

OFFICIAL STATE MAP: C-5
DAWES COUNTY

Nebraska State Historical Society
1860s' painting by W. H. Jackson, "Fording the South Platte"

Located: I-80 East - Big
Springs Rest Area.

OFFICIAL STATE MAP: J-9
DEUEL COUNTY

NEBRASKA
HISTORICAL MARKER

THE GREAT PLATTE RIVER ROAD

Since 1841, Nebraska's Platte River Valley has been the historic highway
of westward migration. In this area, the overland trail divided into two
branches, one which followed the North and the other the South Forks of
the River. Emigrants bound for Oregon or California crossed the South
Platte near here and proceeded up the North Platte Valley past such
milestones as Chimney Rock and Scott's Bluffs. After gold was discovered
in the Rocky Mountains in 1859, an increasing number of travelers
followed the South Fork of the Platte to Denver and the mining camps.

Although the South Platte could be forded at several points, most
frequently used was the "Old California Crossing," several miles east of
present Big Springs. No matter which crossing was chosen, the wide,
sandy river proved a formidable obstacle for the emigrants and their
heavily laden wagons.

Today, the Platte Valley remains an important thoroughfare across
Nebraska and the Nation. A few miles east of here I-80 divides into two
major routes, recalling the role of the South Platte Region as a junction for
overland travel in the 19th Century.

Located: I-80 East - Big
Springs Rest Area.

OFFICIAL STATE MAP: J-9
DEUEL COUNTY

NEBRASKA
HISTORICAL MARKER

BIG SPRINGS

The history of Big Springs, northeast of here, has been closely associated with the Union Pacific Railroad since 1867, when a station was established at that point. A nearby spring, from which the station derived its name, provided an abundant water supply for the railroad's steam locomotives.

On the night of September 18, 1877, Nebraska's most famous train robbery occurred at Big Springs. After capturing the station agent and destroying the telegraph, Sam Bass and five companions stopped a Union Pacific express train and escaped with a reported sixty-thousand dollars in gold and currency.

No permanent settlement occurred at Big Springs until 1883, and the townsite was platted by the Union Pacific Railroad the following year. One of the first structures in the community was the Phelps Hotel, opened in 1885 by Mrs. Sarah Phelps. Little changed since its construction, the hotel has been listed on the National Register of Historic Places.

Despite drouths and severe winters, settlement of the area continued in the 1880's and 1890's. On May 15, 1917, the village of Big Springs was incorporated by act of the Deuel County Commissioners.

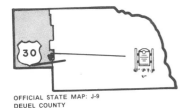

OFFICIAL STATE MAP: J-9
DEUEL COUNTY

Located: US 30 - Railroad
Park in Big Springs.

Sam Bass, in his twenties.

$1,000 Reward!

WE WILL PAY FIVE HUNDRED DOLLARS FOR THE
Arrest and Detention
UNTIL HE CAN BE REACHED, OF

Tom Nixon,

Alias TOM BARNES, five feet seven or eight inches high, 145 to 150 lbs. weight, 25 years of age, blue-gray eyes, light hair and whiskers; beard not heavy or long; mustache older and longer than beard. He is a blacksmith, and worked at that trade in the Black Hills, last summer; has friends in Minnesota and Indiana. He was one of the robbers of the Union Pacific Train, at Big Springs, Nebraska, on September 18, 1877.

He had about $10,000 in $20 Gold pieces of the stolen money in his possession, of the coinage of the San Francisco Mint of 1877. The above reward will be paid for his arrest and detention, and 10 per cent. of all moneys recovered; previous rewards as regards him are withdrawn.

ANY INFORMATION LEADING TO HIS APPREHENSION WILL BE REWARDED. Address,

ALLAN PINKERTON,
CHICAGO, ILLINOIS.
191 and 193 Fifth Avenue,
Or, **E. M. MORSMAN,**
Supt. U. P. R. R. Express.
OMAHA, NEBRASKA.

Nebraska State Historical Society
Sam Bass' wanted poster

NEBRASKA
HISTORICAL MARKER

SAM BASS AND THE BIG SPRINGS ROBBERY

The first and greatest robbery of a Union Pacific train took place near here on the night of September 18, 1877. The legendary Sam Bass and five companions, after capturing John Barnhart, stationmaster, and destroying the telegraph, forced Union Pacific express train No. 4 to halt.

A reported $60,000 in new $20 gold pieces and currency was taken from the express car, while about a thousand dollars and a number of watches were taken from passengers. The accumulated loot from this, the Big Springs Robbery, it is said, was then divided by the outlaws, beneath the Lone Tree then growing on the north side of the river. After making the division, the robbers then split into pairs and fled their pursuers.

Joel Collins and Bill Heffridge were killed at Buffalo, Kansas. Jim Berry was killed near Mexico, Missouri, while Tom Nixon and Jim Davis were never located. After forming another band and robbing four trains in Texas, Sam Bass was killed by Texas Rangers at Round Rock, Texas, on July 21, 1878; it was his 27th birthday. His epitaph reads ''A Brave Man Reposes in Death Here. Why was He not true?''

NEBRASKA
HISTORICAL MARKER

JULESBERG AND FORT SEDGWICK

Julesburg, Colorado, visible to the southwest, was established as a road ranche, trading post and stage station in 1859. Located near the junction of several overland routes, Old Julesburg became an important transportation and military center during the 1860's.

Although a small military garrison, Camp Rankin, was established near Julesburg in 1864, the small military force was unable to prevent over five hundred Sioux and Cheyenne from burning the settlement and killing eighteen defenders on January 7, 1865. Julesburg was rebuilt on a new site, and the military post was enlarged and later renamed Fort Sedgwick.

Until 1871 when it was abandoned, Fort Sedgwick served as a focal point for military activities in the region, and, during the construction of the Union Pacific across western Nebraska in 1867, troops from the post protected the construction workers from the continual threat of Indian attack. At that time, Julesburg was rebuilt near the railroad, and, though it lasted less than a year, it became noted for vice and violence.

The fourth and present Julesburg was platted as Denver Junction in 1884. Two years later, when incorporated, it was renamed Julesburg.

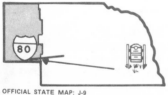

OFFICIAL STATE MAP: J-9
DEUEL COUNTY

Located: I-80 East - Big Springs Rest Area.

Site of Julesberg

Nebraska State Historical Society

Nebraska State Historical Society

Looking south — Oregon Trail

STATE
HISTORICAL
PARK

Located: US 26 - 1 mile south
and east of Lewellen.

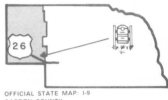

OFFICIAL STATE MAP: I-9
GARDEN COUNTY

NEBRASKA
HISTORICAL MARKER

ASH HOLLOW

Ash Hollow was famous on the Oregon Trail. A branch of the trail ran northwestward from the Lower California Crossing of the South Platte River a few miles west of Brule, and descended here into the North Platte Valley. The hollow, named for a growth of ash trees, was entered by Windlass Hill to the south. Wagons had to be eased down its steep slope by ropes.

Ash Hollow with its water, wood and grass was a welcome relief after the arduous trip from the South Platte and the travelers usually stopped for a period of rest and refitting. An abandoned trappers cabin served as an unofficial postoffice where letters were deposited to be carried to the ''States'' by Eastbound travelers. The graves of Rachel Pattison and other emigrants are in the nearby cemetery.

In 1855 a significant fight, commonly called the Battle of Ash Hollow, occurred at Blue Water Creek northwest of here. General Harney's forces sent out to chastize the Indians after the Grattan Massacre of 1854 here attacked Little Thunder's band of Brule Sioux while the Indians were attempting to parley, killed a large number and captured the rest of the band.

STATE
HISTORICAL
PARK

Nebraska Game and Parks Commission

Aerial view of the road westbound Conestoga wagons cut in 1800's in Ash Hollow.

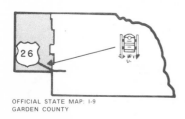

OFFICIAL STATE MAP: I-9
GARDEN COUNTY

Located: US 26 - south and east of Lewellen.

NEBRASKA
HISTORICAL MARKER

ASH HOLLOW GEOLOGY

Ash Hollow is a focal point for understanding the geologic history of the Central Great Plains prior to the onset of the Great Ice Age. It is the type locality of the Ash Hollow Formation, named by Henry Engelmann after a visit in 1858-1859. These sediments were deposited in ancient valley-systems that drained east from the Rocky Mountains.

Much of the ancient valley-fill is exposed in cross section in the cliff faces along Ash Hollow. The basal pebble-gravel forms the roof of Ash Hollow Cave in the exhibit area. Some of the overlying hard ledges or mortar-beds probably represent hard-pan or caliche soils, and others contain fossil grass seeds and root-casts of yucca, all indicative of a semi-arid climate and plants somewhat like today. But the animals found in these rocks were very different, including camels, rhinoceroses, and long-jawed masto-donts, most of which became extinct before the Ice Age. The Ice Age animals were likewise mostly distinct from those now living here.

The earliest collections of fossils were made for E. D. Cope near here in 1879. Explorers who made geological contributions include John C. Fremont in 1843 and G. K. Warren in 1855.

Ash Hollow
State Historical Park

STATE HISTORICAL PARK

Ash Hollow State Historical Park on U.S. Highway 26 east of Lewellen, was formed from another famous stop on the Oregon Trail, as well as being an important prehistoric site. Ash Hollow Cave, first excavated in the 1930's, documents a period of Indian culture about the era of the beginning of Christianity. Reproductions of the artifacts of early North Americans are on display in a unique interpretive building enclosing the cave.

Another historical area near Ash Hollow is the Blue Water Battlefield, site of the first confrontation between the Sioux Indians and the U.S. Army. Still undeveloped, the area is located north of Lewellen.

Located: US 26 - south and east of Lewellen.

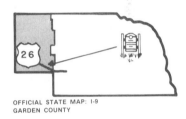

OFFICIAL STATE MAP: I-9
GARDEN COUNTY

Nebraska State Historical Society

Looking north on to Harney Battle site

Thousands of white-masted prairie schooners etched their passing into the sod of Ash Hollow, many passing this new interpretive center located near Lewellen. Here, the legends of the frontier were reality, and 20th Century travelers can actually see the ruts carved by the westward-bound Conestogas.

Nebraska Game and Parks Commission

Nebraska State Historical Society

View north of Windlass Hill

Located: US 26 - 5½ miles
east of Lewellen.

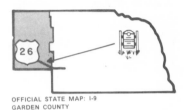

OFFICIAL STATE MAP: I-9
GARDEN COUNTY

NEBRASKA
HISTORICAL MARKER

WINDLASS HILL PIONEER HOMESTEAD

The stones surrounding this marker are the remains of the homestead dwelling of Reverend Dennis B. Clary, a pioneer Methodist Minister, who received final patent for his homestead May 22, 1899. Mr. Clary was born September 1st, 1822, in Maryland and immigrated to Nebraska in 1885. Using a horse drawn cart fashioned from available materials, he hauled stone to this site for a two room house. For years this was a land mark in Ash Hollow and marked the location of Windlass Hill. It was a popular stopping place for settlers traveling from the North Platte Valley area to the railroad at Big Springs, some twenty miles to the south.

The wagon road used at that time is still visible nearby. The Oregon Trail passed here, and the area surrounding the house was used by early travelers to repair damages caused by the hazardous trip down Windlass Hill.

This site was used July 29 - 30, 1967, as the stage setting for the ''Ash Hollow Centennial Pageant'' when a nearby sod house was reconstructed. Funds from this successful historical event provided this Marker.

NATIONAL
HISTORIC
SITE

Sketch of Chimney Rock by Frederick Piercy, 1853   Nebraska State Historical Society

Chimney Rock early 1900's photograph   Nebraska State Historical Society

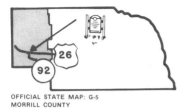

Located: US 26 and Nebraska 92 - 1½ miles southwest of Bayard.

NATIONAL HISTORIC SITE

NEBRASKA HISTORICAL MARKER

CHIMNEY ROCK

No single sight along the Oregon and Mormon trails attracted more attention than Chimney Rock, 1½ miles south of here. Rising 475 feet above the Platte River, the natural tower served as a beacon to pioneers.

Tired travelers described it in many ways during the three to four days it was part of their horizon. For some it created mirage-like effects. Some judged it to be 50 feet high, others 700. Many tried to scale it, but none succeeded. Later it became the setting for pony express, telegraph, and stage stations.

Many pioneers speculated on the fragility of the tower. They feared the Brule clay with interlayers of volcanic ash and Arikaree sandstone would soon crumble to nothingness on the prairie.

Hundreds of names were scratched on the soft base. The names have washed away, but the tower remains, as do references in faded diaries that attest Chimney Rock was one of the celebrated landmarks on the pioneer trunklines to the west.

Chimney Rock still stands tall in 1972 after a hundred years of wind and weather.

Nebraska State Historical Society

Scotts Bluff
National Monument of America

Scotts Bluff is a massive promontory rising 800 feet above the valley floor and 4,649 feet above sea level. Named for Hiram Scott, a fur trapper who died in the vicinity about 1828, the bluff is an ancient landmark and was noted by the earliest tribes whose records have been preserved. To the Indians of the Plains, Scotts Bluff was Me-a-pa-te, or "the-hill-that-is-hard-to-go-around."

The bluff was once part of the ancient High Plains. Erosion over long periods has cut down the surrounding valleys to their present level, leaving Scotts Bluff and the adjoining hills as remnants of the unbroken plains which now lie farther to the west.

The North Platte Valley, of which Scotts Bluff is the dominant natural feature, has been a human migration corridor for centuries. Some stone artifacts found here indicate that man has been here for more than 10,000 years. When white men first arrived, they found that this area was a favorite hunting ground of Sioux, Cheyenne, and Arapaho Indians, for here vast herds of buffalo came to water.

The first white men to see Scotts Bluff were Robert Stuart and his companions, who in 1812-13 passed by carrying dispatches to John Jacob Astor from his new fur post in Oregon. In the years that followed, trappers and traders saw it when they brought their beaver pelts down the Platte River to settlements farther east; and explorers and missionaries passed

OFFICIAL STATE MAP: G-4
SCOTTS BLUFF COUNTY

Located: US 26 - 5 miles southwest of Scottsbluff.

Park Headquarters Complex

National Park Service

194

the bluff on their way from advance posts of civilization into the western wilderness.

In 1843 the vanguard of a great pioneer army passed Scotts Bluff in the first large migration to Oregon. Four years later Brigham Young led the first group of his followers past the bluff on the north side of the Platte, a route later famous as the Mormon Trail. The 2 years following the discovery of gold in California in 1848 saw more than 150,000 men, women, and children traveling through the area.

In 1860-61 Pony Express riders galloped through Mitchell Pass. They were followed shortly by the first transcontinental telegraph. The Overland Mail, Pony Express, Pacific Telegraph, and Overland Stage built stations near Scotts Bluff. In 1864 Fort Mitchell was established 2½ miles to the northwest to protect stagecoaches and wagon trains on the Oregon Trail. The following year the North Platte Valley was considered as a possible route for the Union Pacific, then building westward to link up with the Central Pacific to form the first transcontinental railroad, but a line through Cheyenne was chosen instead. The completion of the railroad in 1869 marked the decline of the Oregon Trail, although it continued in use locally for many years.

In the late 1870's and early 1880's, Scotts Bluff was the geographical center of the open-range cattle industry, the last great romantic episode of the frontier. With the arrival of the first homesteaders in the North Platte Valley in 1885, the local frontier disappeared and Scotts Bluff became a symbol of the Nation's past.

National Park Service

NATIONAL MONUMENT

POINTS OF INTEREST

The visitor center contains exhibits telling the story of the westward migration and recalling Scotts Bluff's role as a landmark on the Oregon and Mormon Trails. Paintings by William Henry Jackson, the famous pioneer photographer and artist who followed the Oregon Trail as a bullwhacker in 1866, are also displayed.

The Summit Self-guiding Trail, extending to the north and south overlooks from the summit parking area, is 0.6 of a mile long, hard surfaced, and an easy grade. From the north overlook there is a panorama of the North Platte Valley, highlighted by several famous landmarks: Chimney Rock, 25 miles to the east, and Laramie Peak, 100 miles to the west. From the south overlook, you look down on the Oregon Trail approach to Mitchell Pass. The summit trail offers other grand vistas.

Oregon Trail. Except for intermittent stretches of cultivation or where modern roads have been superimposed, the trough of the old trail, ground down by the passage of a million emigrants, can still be seen from the transmonument road south of the east entrance, across from the visitor center, and in Mitchell Pass. From the visitor center, you can walk along the Oregon Trail to the site where William H. Jackson camped in 1866.

Dome Rock as viewed from the west   National Park Service

196

National Park Service

A typical scene on the Oregon Trail with Volunteers in Parks, VIPS, preparing an evening meal over a campfire of buffalo chips and cedar wood. During the tourist season VIPS perform other living history demonstrations.

REBECCA WINTERS

Rebecca Winters, daughter of Gideon Burdick, a drummer boy in Washington's army, was born in New York State in 1802. She was a pioneer in the Church of the Latter Day Saints, being baptized with her husband Hiram in June 1833.

Membership in the Church brought persecution in Ohio, Illinois and Iowa. In June 1852 the family joined others of their faith in the great journey to Utah. It was a pleasant trip across Iowa through June, but in the Platte Valley the dread cholera struck. Rebecca saw many of her friends taken by the illness, and on August 15 she was another of its victims. She was buried on the prairie near here with a simple ceremony.

A close friend of the family, William Reynolds, chiseled the words "Rebecca Winters, age 50" on an iron wagon tire to mark the grave. The family continued on with the wagon train and settled in Pleasant Grove, Utah.

Burlington Railroad surveyors found the crude marker and changed the right-of-way to save and protect the grave. In 1902 a monument was erected by Rebecca's descendants. Rebecca Winters is a symbol of the pioneer mother who endured great hardships in the westward movement.

Located: US 26 - 2 miles south of Scottsbluff.

OFFICIAL STATE MAP: G-4
SCOTTS BLUFF COUNTY

Rebecca Winters' grave with some of her oldest and youngest living descendants

Nebraska State Historical Society

Located: Nebraska 27 - 30 miles south of Gordon near a lake.

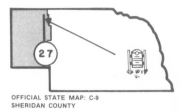

OFFICIAL STATE MAP: C-9
SHERIDAN COUNTY

NEBRASKA
HISTORICAL MARKER

MARI SANDOZ
1896-1966

This is the country of Mari Sandoz--historian, novelist, teacher--who brought its history and its people to life in her many books, articles and stories. She was born in Sheridan County, Nebraska. Although she lived much of her life in the East, she is buried here in her own West.

Mari Sandoz was first famed for **Old Jules** (1935), the story of her father and other settlers who came to the upper Niobrara region in the late nineteenth century. Her greatest achievement is the series of the six related books on life as it developed with Indian and white man in the trans-Missouri country: **The Beaver Man, Crazy Horse, Cheyenne Autumn, The Buffalo Hunters, The Cattlemen** and **Old Jules**. In these and a dozen other volumes she presented the drama of man on the Great Plains more completely, accurately and vividly than anyone before her had done.

Mari Sandoz was internationally known as a chronicler of the West and as an expert on Indian history. Her own aim was to understand all of life by understanding this one part of it: how man shaped the Plains country, and how it shaped him.

Nebraska State Historical Society

Mari Sandoz

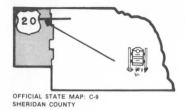

OFFICIAL STATE MAP: C-9
SHERIDAN COUNTY

Located: US 20 - west of Gordon.

E. S. Newman

Nebraska State Historical Society

NEBRASKA
HISTORICAL MARKER

OPENING THE SANDHILLS

The first ranch in this area was set up on the Niobrara River about five miles south of here in 1877. E. S. Newman established his ranch to sell cattle to the government for delivery to the Indians at the Pine Ridge Agency to the north.

The sandhills, later to become the heart of Nebraska's cattle country, were shunned by Newman and his contemporaries who set up ranches on their edge. The cattlemen believed the region of shifting sand dunes, with few streams or other known sources of water, would not support cattle and was even dangerous for humans.

In the spring of 1879, Newman and his fellow ranchers were forced to enter the sandhills hoping to salvage a small portion of the stock that had drifted south of the Niobrara River in the severe winter storms. They found the cattle had both shelter and good grass and water in the hills. Since then Nebraska's sandhills have acquired a thicker and more stable covering of grass. This rolling country with its plentiful vegetation and its diamond-like lakes nestled between the hills has become one of the most productive cattle-raising regions in the world.

Agate Fossil Beds
National Monument of America

NATIONAL
MONUMENT

Here at Agate Fossil Beds National Monument are concentrated the fossils of animals in beds of sedimentary rock, formed, about 20 million years ago, by the compression of mud, clay, and erosional materials deposited by the action of water and wind. These species of animals, then so numerous, have long been extinct. The beds, which acquired their name from their proximity to rock formations containing agates, are under the grass-covered Carnegie and University Hills. From the summits of these hills, named by early collecting parties, you can look down on the lazy meanders of the Niobrara River, 200 feet below.

Early pioneers of scientific research in the West centered many of their activities here. Capt. James H. Cook was the first white man to discover fossil bones at Agate Fossil Beds, about 1878. Since then, bones from the site have been exhibited throughout the world. Captain Cook and his son, Harold, made Agate Springs Ranch a headquarters for paleontologists and acquired an excellent fossil collection.

AGATE FOSSIL BEDS TODAY

Scientists estimate that at least 75 percent of the fossil-bearing parts of the hills are unquarried. The Miocene fossil mammal bones are extremely abundant, comprise a variety of different species, and are remarkably well preserved, with numerous complete skeletons.

Except for livestock that graze on the hills which relieve the comparatively flat open valley of the Niobrara River, the scene is relatively undisturbed.

The landscape is carpeted predominantly with grasses such as prairie sandreed, blue grama, little bluestem, and needle-and-thread. The prairie flowers—lupine, spiderwort, western wallflower, sunflower, and penste-

Located: US 29 - 34 miles north of Mitchell.

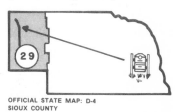

OFFICIAL STATE MAP: D-4
SIOUX COUNTY

University and Carnegie Hills viewed from the northwest in Agate Fossil Beds National Monument.

National Park Service

mon—add color to this grassland scene. Small soapweed, a yucca, growing on the hillsides, is particularly attractive, especially in late summer when its dark green spears stand out among the brown grass.

Cottonwoods and willows along the river add to the attractiveness of the scene and supply resting places and shelter for birds and other animals.

Animals are typical of the western plains: mule deer, pronghorn, coyote, cottontail, and prairie rattlesnake.

DEVELOPMENT OF AGATE FOSSIL BEDS

The Service plans to expose representative fossil remains at Carnegie and University Hills by removing the layers of sediments above the 2- to 3-foot thick horizontal fossil beds. You will then be able to see the fossil skeletons of many creatures just as they were buried millions of years ago, and feel closely associated with the now-extinct animals of a past age. Here, too, you will have an opportunity to watch scientists exposing the deposits, reconstructing some of the skeletons, and reliefing certain deposits in place.

Plans call for interpretive structures at major points of interest and for permanent buildings at the headquarters site. Roads, trails, and a bridge across the Niobrara River will provide access to these points.

GEOLOGY OF THE FOSSIL SITE

The Agate site contains an outstanding record of a chapter of evolution frequently referred to as the Age of Mammals because of the tremendous increase in species and numbers of mammals during that period.

All of Agate's fossil deposits are found in what geologists call the Arikaree Group of the Miocene Epoch, which spanned the period from 25 to 13 million years ago. The group is in turn divided into three formations—Gering, Monroe Creek, and Harrison. The Harrison beds contain practically all of the known fossils at this site. The sedimentary rocks of this group are principally sandstone. The quarries are in the lower part of the Harrison, and the "devil's corkscrews"—casts of ancient

This in-situ display on Carnegie Hill shows relief bones in bone bed.

National Park Service

NATIONAL MONUMENT

National Park Service

Devil's Corkscrew formations, spiral fossil casts, are generally 6 to 8 feet high and from 3 to 8 inches in diameter.

beaver burrows—are in the upper part, which was laid down perhaps a million or more years after the lower part of the formation.

ANCIENT LIFE

By far the most common mammal at Agate Fossil Beds was the **Diceratherium**, a two-horned rhinoceros. This fleetfooted grazer was smaller than a Shetland pony, and roamed the plains in numbers as great as those of our bison before 1850.

The most unusual looking animal was the **Moropus**, a large, heavily built mammal about 7 feet at the shoulders. The head was horselike, the neck suggested faintly a giraffe, the torso a tapir, the front legs a rhinoceros, and the hindlegs a bear. Most unusual were the feet, which were armed with large claws used for defense and for digging up roots and bulbs.

Perhaps the most ferocious was the **Dinohyus**, or "Terrible Pig"—a monstrous beast more than 7 feet tall at the shoulders and about 10 feet long. It had a massive head with large tusks and a small brain. However, unlike our domestic pig, its legs were quite long and slender. It was apparently an aggressive creature and was frequently wounded in battle.

Large herds of a delicate, graceful little mammal the **Stenomylus**—roamed the Miocene plains. It was slightly over 2 feet tall and had long, slender legs and deerlike hooves.

Fragments of fossils have been found of many other animals that lived here during the Miocene Epoch.

THE FOSSIL-COLLECTING STORY

In the summer of 1904, O. A. Peterson of the Carnegie Museum at Pittsburgh came to Agate, and with the able assistance of Harold Cook, then 17, conducted the first scientific excavation at this site. They discovered a rich quarry, containing a type of rhinoceros that was new to science.

In 1905, Prof. E. H. Barbour and four students of the University of Nebraska opened a quarry in the side of University Hill. Both the Carnegie Museum and the University of Nebraska worked their respective quarries for a number of collecting seasons. Yale University also collected at the quarries about the same time.

In 1906, Prof. E. B. Loomis and a party from Amherst College joined the collectors. They excavated in a small hill which Loomis called Amherst Point. Returning in 1907 and again in 1908, the Loomis party discovered a quarry of **Stenomylus** skeletons. Approximately 18 skulls, together with enough scattered bones to complete the skeletons, were collected from one pocket. In an adjacent area, three complete skeletons were found.

In 1909, the Carnegie Museum removed at least 40 skeletons. The American Museum of Natural History collected here for about 20 years,

starting in 1910.

Several other institutions sent collecting parties to Agate in later years. The last excavation was made at the **Stenomylus** quarry in 1950 by the South Dakota School of Mines and Technology.

THE COOK FAMILY

To learn how this site in the valley of the Niobrara became one of such intense interest, you must know something about the Cook family.

Capt. James H. Cook acquired the Agate Springs Ranch in 1887 from his father-in-law, Dr. E. B. Graham, who had established it a few years earlier as the 0-4 Ranch.

At 16, James left his home in Michigan and became a cowboy riding herd on unpredictable Texas longhorns on long cattle drives from Mexico to Montana. He was a big game hunter and guide in 1878 in Wyoming and later in New Mexico.

Captain Cook served with distinction as a scout attached to the 8th U.S. Cavalry in New Mexico during the campaign of 1885-86 against the famous Apache chieftain, Geronimo. During this service, he married Kate Graham; he settled for the rest of his life at the Agate Springs Ranch, which once had been part of the Sioux Indian lands.

Cook had made friends with Professors E. D. Cope and O. C. Marsh, who were two of the world's most renowned palentologists. Because of his associations with them and other prominent scientists, he became keenly interested in this field.

He was looked upon by the Indians as a friend; because of this, he acquired a large collection of Indian artifacts. Best known of his Indian friends was Red Cloud, the daring Sioux Chieftain.

ABOUT YOUR VISIT

Monument headquarters, between the Niobrara River and the county road, is about 3 miles east of Agate Springs Ranch. The temporary visitor center has exhibits on the fossil story, and nearby is a self-guiding trail to an area of exposed fossils.

Private collecting of fossils, rocks or plants is now forbidden by law.

ADMINISTRATION

Agate Fossil Beds National Monument, the establishment of which was authorized on June 5, 1965, is administered by the National Park Service, U.S. Department of the Interior.

The monument, consisting of approximately 1,970 acres, is irregular in shape. A small detached area of 60 acres containing the **Stenomylus** quarry is included.

This is an exhibit at the University of Nebraska State Museum.

National Park Service

Nebraska State Historical Society

Cheyenne Tepees

Located: US 20 - 1 mile southwest of Fort Robinson.

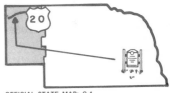

OFFICIAL STATE MAP: C-4
SIOUX COUNTY

NEBRASKA
HISTORICAL MARKER

THE CHEYENNE OUTBREAK

On September 9, 1878, after a year of suffering on an Oklahoma reservation, some 300 Northern Cheyenne Indians began a trek back to their homeland. Dull Knife's band of 149 Indians were captured and taken to Fort Robinson. For months they refused to return to their hated reservation.

Captain Wessels, Commanding Officer at Fort Robinson, imprisoned the Indians in a log barracks and attempted to starve them into submission. Using the few weapons they had smuggled into the building, the younger warriors began the Cheyenne Outbreak about 9:00 p.m., January 9, 1879. After a desperate running battle on the snow-covered parade ground, the Indians managed to follow the banks of the White River, scale the cliffs and escape.

Unable to find horses, the Cheyenne eluded pursuing troops for 12 days by heading northwest through the rough terrain of the Pine Ridge. Soldiers discovered their hiding place on Antelope Creek January 22, but the Indians refused to surrender. During the outbreak, 64 Cheyenne and 11 soldiers were killed. More than 70 were recaptured and several escaped. The number of casualties made the Cheyenne Outbreak one of the major conflicts of the Indian Wars.

General P.N. Sheridan   Nebraska State Historical Society

Spotted Tail   Nebraska State Historical Society

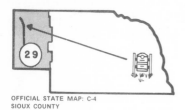

OFFICIAL STATE MAP: C-4
SIOUX COUNTY

Located: US 29 - south of Harrison, north of Agate.

NEBRASKA
HISTORICAL ⬡ MARKER

FORT LARAMIE--FORT ROBINSON TRAIL

Near here are ruts left by the famed 1874 Sioux Expedition, a U.S. military force sent to establish Camps Sheridan and Robinson. The 1868 Treaty of Fort Laramie had guaranteed food and supplies to the Sioux and other tribes in exchange for lands ceded to the United States. To distribute annuity goods, Red Cloud Agency was established on the North Platte River below Fort Laramie. In 1873 the agency was relocated to the White River Valley near present-day Crawford.

Misunderstandings between Indian leaders and agents hampered the distribution of supplies during the winter of 1873-1874. In three separate incidents in February, hostile bands of Sioux killed freighter Edward Gray, Red Cloud agent Frank Appleton, and two soldiers from Fort Laramie, including Lieutenant Levi Robinson. General Philip Sheridan responded by organizing the Sioux Expedition.

In early March nearly one thousand troops followed an old fur-trade route from Fort Laramie to the Red Cloud and Spotted Tail Agencies. The establishment of Camps Robinson and Sheridan maintained an uneasy peace until the outbreak of the Sioux War two years later. Camp Robinson was renamed Fort Robinson in 1878 and the improved Fort Laramie--Fort Robinson Trail helped supply this outpost on the plains.

County Index

Illustration Index

Illustration Index

Illustration Index

General Index

General Index

General Index

General Index

General Index

General Index

General Index

General Index

General Index

OMAHA - 26, 27, 29, 64, 66, 72, 95-98, 99, 132, 140
"Omaha", meaning of - 106
Omaha Creek - 19
Omaha-Fort Kearney state route - 68
Omaha High School - 27
Omaha Indians - 9, 15, 19, 75, 99, 106, 107
Omaha Indian village - 19
Omaha, Niobrara and Black Hills Railroad - 88
Omaha Reservation - 107
OMAHA TRIBE - 106
Omohundro, Texas Jack - 135
OPENING THE SANDHILLS - 200
"Open range" - 141
Ord, Nebraska - 166-168, 170
Ord, General O. E. C. - 166-168
Ordinance Sergeant - 93
Oregon - 2, 50-53, 150, 155, 157, 183, 192, 194-197
OREGON TRAIL, THE - 2, 13, 44-47, 50-53, 69, 77, 78, 86, 102, 130, 131, 156, 157, 187, 189-190, 191, 193, 194-197
Orient - 7
Orleans - 141
Osage Indians - 120
Osceola, Nebraska - 90
OSCEOLA AND THE EARLY PIONEER - 90
Oto Indians - 19, 75, 99, 102, 103, 104, 110
Oto Indian territory - 104
OTO MISSION - 103
Oto Village - 103
Outpost - 93, 110, 112-114
"Outpost on the plains" - 181, 206
Overland Mail - 194-197
Overland routes - 2, 88, 146, 157, 186
Overland stages - 50-53, 194-197
Overland Trail - 38, 93, 150, 155, 158, 183
Overland travel - 78, 146, 176, 183
Overseas export - 3
Ox-Bow Trail - 80, 104
Oxford, Nebraska - 138

P

Pacific City, Nebraska - 18
Pacific Ocean - 132
Pacific Telegraph - 194-197
Pa-huk Hill - 22, 120
Palentologists - 201-204
Palmer-Epard cabin - 33-36
Pani Leshar - 89
Panic of 1857 - 108
Panic of 1867 - 101
Papillion, Nebraska - 101
Parker, Samuel - 192
Parkman, Francis - 177, 192
Passageway - 67
Pastors - 18, 100
Patents - 75, 191
Pattison, Rachel - 146, 187
PAWNEE - 71
Pawnee Chief - 89
Pawnee Country - 71
Pawnee Indians - 22, 31, 38, 41, 66, 70, 71, 89, 99, 102, 104, 120, 130, 142, 165, 166-168
Pawnee Indian Agency - 70
Pawnee Indian Reservation - 70, 89, 166-168
Pawnee Killer - 133
Pawnee Ranch - 77
Pawnee Royalty Company - 91
Pawnee sacred places - 22, 120
Pawnee Scouts - 22, 71, 89, 130, 156
PAWNEE VILLAGE - 66, 104
Pawnee War of 1859 - 66
Peace conferences - 104, 120
Pebble Creek - 165, 166-168
Pebble-gravel - 188
Pennsylvania - 33-36, 170, 201-204
Pennsylvania steel mills - 23
Perkins County - 159
Pershing, John J. - 126
PERU STATE COLLEGE - 76
Petalesharo - 22, 71
Peterson, O. A. - 201-204
PHELPS COUNTY - 85, 130, 131

Phelps Hotel - 184
Phelps, Mrs. Sarah - 184
Phillipson, A. E. - 137
Photographer - 194-197
Pierre, S. D. - 175
Pike, Lt. Zeublon M. - 120
Pilcher, Joshua - 192
Pile, Professor James M. - 115, 116
Pilger, Nebraska - 105
Pilger, Peter - 105
Pine Ridge - 205
Pine Ridge Agency - 182, 200
PIONEER CROSSING - 43
Pioneer Gallery - 59-61
Pioneer heritage - 16
PIONEER PARK - 41
Pittsburgh, Pennsylvania - 201-204
Plains Indians - 59-61, 71, 194-197
Plains Woodland people - 9
Platte County - 87
Platte River - 2, 6, 22, 38, 39, 49, 55, 67, 68, 69, 71, 77, 78, 79, 85, 86, 102, 103, 128, 130, 131, 135, 146, 150, 156, 157, 160, 166-168, 193
Platte River Road - 146, 147, 150, 157, 158
Platte Valley - 2, 37, 40, 80, 86, 88, 99, 102, 146, 150, 155, 156, 157, 166-168, 183, 192, 198
Pleasant Grove, Utah - 198
Pleasant Hill, Nebraska - 94
Plum Creek, Nebraska - 130
Plum Creek Massacre - 85, 86, 130, 131
Poet Laureate of Nebraska - 15, 115, 116
Pole Cat - 133
Polish immigrants - 88
Polk County - 90
PONCA - 21
PONCA INDIANS - 4, 17, 21, 56, 99
Ponca Reservation - 4
Ponca State Park - 21
Ponca "Trail of Tears" - 4
Pony Express - 2, 44-47, 50-53, 54, 86, 102, 130, 131, 150, 151-154, 157, 158, 176, 193, 194-197
"Post on the North Fork of the Loup River" - 165
Post office - 13, 20, 40, 41, 62, 88, 90, 127, 141, 172, 187
Pottery - 9, 71
Powder River Campaigns - 89
Powell, Major John Wesley - 132
Prague, Nebraska - 92
Prague - 92
Prairie DuChien Treaty - 75
Prairie fires - 5, 18, 30, 68, 112-114, 163
Prairie flowers - 201-204
Prairie grasses - 201-204
Prairie highway - 2
Prehistoric site - 189-190
Preakness - 29
Presbyterian Church of Nebraska - 100
Preuss, Charles - 192
Prince Maximilian - 99
Printing office - 78
Proclamations - 32, 117
Professors - 201-204
Prohibition Party of Nebraska - 74
Province of Bohemia - 92
Publisher - 74

Q

Quarries - 49, 201-204
Queen's Plate - 29

R

Race tracks - 10, 21
Rainfall - 42, 131, 132
Rains - 4, 138
Ranch 1733 - 6
Range land - 164
"Rattlesnake Ed" - 149
Real estate - 74
REBECCA WINTERS - 198
Ream, James D. - 129
Recreation areas - 21, 138, 180

217

General Index

General Index

Sod House Frontier - 59-61, 127
Soil conditions - 10, 42, 138, 155
Soil Conservation Society of America - 139
So-Lite Flour - 3
Soldier's Free Homestead Colony - 5
"Song of Years" - 11
South China Sea - 57
South Dakota School of Mines and Technology - 201-204
South Fork River - 138
South Loup Valley - 166-168
South Platte River - 150, 157, 159, 183, 187
Southern Ponca Indians - 56
Spalding, Elizabeth - 158
Spanish settlers - 19, 67, 120
Spearfish, S. D. - 170
Special Exhibits Gallery - 59-61
Spirk, J. W. - 3
"Splendid Wayfaring" - 15
Spotted Tail Agency - 206
"Spring Came on Forever" - 11
SPRING VALLEY PARK - 163
Squadron Commander - 170
Squatters Cabin - 33-36
Stagecoaches - 2, 26, 81-84, 174, 175, 194-197
Stage route - 68
Stage stations - 38, 68, 77, 85, 130, 186, 193
Stanton, Edwin M. - 105
Stanton, Nebraska - 105
STANTON COUNTY - 105
State Archives - 59-61
State Historical Parks - 44-47, 50-53, 81-84, 112-114, 123-125, 151-154, 165, 166-168, 180, 189-190
State Park Board - 180
Statesmen - 161
State-supported college - 76
Steamboats - 23, 79, 109
STEAMBOAT BERTRAND - 109
Steamboat landing - 99, 108
Steam locomotives - 184
"Steam Wagon" - 79, 80
Steam Wagon Road - 79, 80
"Stenomylus quarry" - 201-204
Stinking Water Creek - 159
Stockade - 111, 112-114, 182
STOCKVILLE - 135
Stolley, William - 40
Stone parsonage - 12
Stough, Dr. Solomon B. - 21
Strang, Nebraska - 30
STRATEGIC AEROSPACE MUSEUM - 95-98
Strategic Air Command - 95-98, 99
Strategic Support Aircraft - 95-98
Stuart, Robert - 192, 194-197
Sublette, William - 192
Summit Self-guiding Trail - 194-197
Supply stops - 70
Surreys - 81-84
SUTTON - 14
Sutton, Massachusetts - 14
SWAN CITY - 94
Swan Creek - 94
Swearengen, Jack - 140
Swedish - 30, 85, 104, 105
Swiss Immigrants - 88
Switzerland - 93

T

Table Creek - 50-53, 78, 79
"Tanglefoot" - 54
Tappage Indians - 22, 71
Taylor, W. Z. - 141
Teachers colleges - 115, 116, 179
Telegraph - 26, 40, 50-53, 73, 86, 102, 130, 131, 184, 185, 193, 194-197
Tennessee - 33-36
Tennessee Valley Authority - 161
TERRITORIAL CHURCH - 18
Territorial Legislature - 21, 62
Territorial Secretary - 66
Teton Sioux Indians - 166-168
Texas - 55, 134, 145, 159, 185

Texas Longhorn Cattle - 126, 134, 141, 148, 149, 150, 159, 201-204
Texas Rangers - 185
TEXAS TRAIL, THE - 159
Texas - (Ogallala) Trail - 134, 148, 149, 150, 159
TEXAS TRAIL CANYON - 134
Thayer, General John M. - 22, 66, 104
Thompson, Vic & Maude - 163
Thompson Colony - 31
Thoroughbred horses - 29, 87
Thorp, Colonel John - 5
Timber - 68, 139, 176
Timber claim - 139
Timber Culture Act of 1873 - 139
Tipi poles - 176
Tipton, T.W. - 73
Tobias, Nebraska - 93
TONWANTONGA - 19
Town Hall - 101
"Township Farm" - 105
"Trading house" - 177
Trading posts - 85, 135, 136, 141, 177, 186, 192, 194-197
Trail drives - 134, 148, 159, 201-204
Train robberies - 184, 185
Training aircraft - 95-98, 170
Training center - 181
Training school - 28
Transfer point - 73
Transportation center - 23, 186
Trappers - 2, 140, 158, 192, 194-197
Treaties - 4, 22, 56, 75, 106, 110, 175, 178, 182, 206
Treaty of Fort Laramie - 4, 56, 206
Treaty of Table Creek - 22
Treaty Tree - 178
Trecy, Father Jeremiah - 17
Trecy Colony - 17
Trees - 68, 74, 81-84, 139, 187, 201-204
Trenton, Nebraska - 71, 138, 141
Triple Crown - 29
Turkey Creek - 43
Twentieth Amendment - 161

U

Unicameral Legislature in the State of Nebraska - 161
Union Pacific Railroad - 2, 5, 6, 26, 41, 50-53, 54, 69, 79, 80, 88, 90, 99, 130, 131, 132, 148, 150, 159, 166-168, 174, 175, 176, 184, 185, 186, 194-197
Ulysses, Nebraska - 90
Underground water supplies - 85, 164
U. S. Air Force aircraft - 95-98
U. S. Army - 3, 28, 49, 78, 89, 93, 143, 166-168, 175, 189-190
U. S. Army Dragoons - 66, 192
U. S. Constitution - 161
U. S. Department of Interior - 201-204
U. S. Geological Survey - 132
U. S. House of Representatives - 161
U. S. Land Office - 31, 55
U. S. Post Office - 62, 127
U. S. Secretary of Agriculture - 81-84
U. S. Senate - 73, 161
U. S. Troops - 146, 158, 176, 205
Universities - 26, 65, 162, 180, 201-204
UNIVERSITY OF NEBRASKA, THE - 65, 180, 201-204
University Hall - 65
University Hills - 201-204
USS Frank E. Evans - 57
Utah - 11, 38, 102, 130, 131, 158, 192, 198

V

Valentine, Nebraska - 126
Valentine, E. K. - 126
"Vein of petroleum" - 91
Vermillion, South Dakota - 33-36
Veterans - 5, 33-36, 107, 144
Victor Wild Stakes - 29
Vietnam - 57
Volcanic ash - 193
Volcano - 20

219

General Index

DEC 3 0 1974 S

F667
B73

C56943

Brevet's Nebraska historical markers and sites. Sioux
Falls, S. D. : Brevet Press, 1974.

viii, 220 p. : ill. ; 22 cm.

On spine: Nebraska historical markers & sites.
Includes index.
ISBN 0-88498-020-0. ISBN 0-88498-021-9 pbk.

1. Historical markers—Nebraska. 2. Historic sites—Nebraska.
3. Nebraska—History.   I. Title: Nebraska historical markers &
sites.

F667.B73   917.82'04'3   74–79979
                                                        MARC
Library of Congress   74 [4]

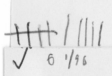

Please Do Not Remove Card From Pocket

YOUR LIBRARY CARD

may be used at all library agencies. You
are, of course, responsible for all materials
checked out on it. As a courtesy to others
please return materials promptly — before
overdue penalties are imposed.

The SAINT PAUL PUBLIC LIBRARY